Twelve
Doorways of Light

A Portal to Your God-Self

SARAH JEANE

BALBOA
PRESS

A DIVISION OF HAY HOUSE

Balboa Press books may be ordered through booksellers or by contacting:

Balboa Press
A Division of Hay House
1663 Liberty Drive
Bloomington, IN 47403
www.balboapress.com
1-(877) 407-4847

Because of the dynamic nature of the Internet, any web addresses or links contained in this book may have changed since publication and may no longer be valid. The views expressed in this work are solely those of the author and do not necessarily reflect the views of the publisher, and the publisher hereby disclaims any responsibility for them.

The author of this book does not dispense medical advice or prescribe the use of any technique as a form of treatment for physical, emotional, or medical problems without the advice of a physician, either directly or indirectly. The intent of the author is only to offer information of a general nature to help you in your quest for emotional and spiritual well-being. In the event you use any of the information in this book for yourself, which is your constitutional right, the author and the publisher assume no responsibility for your actions.

Any people depicted in stock imagery provided by Thinkstock are models, and such images are being used for illustrative purposes only.
Certain stock imagery © Thinkstock.

Print information available on the last page.

ISBN: 978-1-4525-6916-1 (sc)
ISBN: 978-1-4525-6918-5 (hc)
ISBN: 978-1-4525-6917-8 (e)

Library of Congress Control Number: 2013903183

Balboa Press rev. date: 10/16/2015

This book is dedicated to Mother Teresa
and to all Emissaries of Peace.

The Tree of Life

A Representation of our Divine Beingness

METATRON

MELCHIZEDEK

MICHAEL

KETHER
1
Yod-Hay-Vav-Hay
Messenger

BINAH
3
The Infinite Mind
Co-Creator

CHOKMAH
2
Truth
Fool

DA-AT
Ain Sof (front)
Leader
Being (back)
Teacher

GEBURAH
5
Unity
Lover

CHESED
4
In Love
Spirit

TIPHERETH
6
Purity
Healer

HOD
8
Joy
Harmonizer

NETZACH
7
Spirit
Magician

YESOD
9
I Am That I Am
Unifier

MALKUT
10
All That is
Manifestor

This work came into being in furtherance of our global shift in consciousness, in service to the Light encompassing all of creation—in furtherance of world peace and harmony.

In these messages, my joy and life's purpose is to invite you to discover the consciousness of your God-Self, and to rejoice living within that love and light of the heart—revering the sacredness in all life.
This work is inspired by a personal spiritual journey that led me to dedicate my life to bringing together all beings in love, honoring a consciousness of the heart. It is from that place that blissful serenity, wisdom, and harmony are revealed and expressed within the Tree of Life, in you, and in all life.

The Tree of Life of the Cosmos is identified as the "Heart of the Heavens by the Maya", revealing the Tree of Life of the Galaxy and Solar System, and the Tree of Life of the Earth Being. The Tree of Life is present within every human being and within all living organisms all the way to the elementary particles. All levels of the Tree of Life are expressed in the oneness of space and dimensions—and in the heart of all creation.

Throughout this book, I present guidelines and solutions to make peace a living reality by anchoring in the consciousness of our true divine nature, so that we shall know how to love and honor one another—so that we shall know how to honor Mother Earth with all its inhabitants and nature's intelligence—now and always.

I progressively lead the readers into higher and higher consciousness of their divinity and light—their God-Self.

I am inviting you to navigate through timeless, dimensional, divine, creative realities of love, leading to Twelve Doorways of Light—the Tree of Life. This activation is inviting a Portal to your God-Self.

I open the Stargate of my heart, embracing the supreme light in the full realization of my essence.

♥

Messages from the Angels of Light:

In the heavens, the angels invited me to sing with them:
"Om, I am Elohim!"

♥

....And the Angels said:
"All that is of love shall be yours."

♥

"All life is loving, and I bathe myself in that
source of love, now and always."

♥

The Flower of Life

This symbol has been found all around the World.
Its basic synergy is embedded and encoded within the divine design of Life.
The Flower of Life encompasses all divine design intrinsic to all Life
and Creation, such as the Spiral and the Golden Mean.

The Flower of Life encompasses the Tree of Life.
They are sourcing from Creation.

I am releasing into the divine light of God this sacred creative compilation in service to all humanity. This work invites and allows the space for the infinite universal paradigm of the supreme light to radiate in its full divine expression and frequency, sourcing from the Flower of Life, encompassing all elements in nature, all levels of creation and all sacred geometry.

May this creative compilation reach the most profound place of our beingness, so that in oneness, we shall open our hearts to rejoice in the Divine Living Presence!

May the highest qualities of love, reverence, compassion, joy, and gratitude be now recognized and expressed in all hearts—throughout the planet and beyond. May we live in holy consciousness, awakening infinite creative gifts and divine forces of love light sourcing from the heart—navigating within the light of the Tree of Life—to merely know oneness.

May we celebrate life in joy, everlastingly expanding in grace, forever free in the light!

DEDICATION

The world is in need of infinite compassion, grace, and love. In furtherance of global peace, I dedicate these divine messages to all the people of the world, all members of the animal kingdom, nature's intelligence, and the Earth Being—our Mother—in infinite praise and honoring.

All children are in need of nurturing kindness and expression of pure love. This work supports such a path, walking united in joy with our children, with our families, friends and neighbors, and in harmony with the animal kingdom—in the freedom of the light.

This book, this portal of light, is dedicated to Mother Teresa, in boundless reverence and love. Her legacy, faith, and holiness continue to inspire me and guide me in every step of my life, opening my heart to love all beings.
Thank you, Mother Teresa, for your loving spirit forever embracing all beings and all creation, in God's love.

TABLE OF CONTENTS

Chapter Two 61

How to be Free from Guilt, Blame, Judgment,
Jealousy, Animosity, and Resentment •
The Bliss to Forgive • Compassion •
Wishing Love, Joy, Wellness,
and Goodness to Every Being

Chapter Three .87

The Power of Thoughts, Feelings,
Emotions, Beliefs, and Words •
The Power of Gratitude, Joy, and Love

PREFACE

SPECIAL GUIDELINES FOR READERS:

Twelve Doorways of Light epitomizes a holy portal of light—God's divine qualities of love—activating the Stargate of the heart, the Tree of Life within "you" and in all life—for all beings and all life to embrace. This work holds a sacred space for all human beings to move into unity consciousness. When crossing that bridge, true consciousness of unbounded love is revealed, well-being and divine creativity are released in limitless forms and expressions.

These Doorways invite you to navigate within the wonders of life and of your inner being, diving deeper and deeper within the heart of your essence and divine presence.

These messages, inspired from divine guidance, invite qualities of the soul to be experienced—inviting all human expression and limitation to be transcended, allowing a consciousness that is divine and of unconditional love.

If you are searching for increasing awareness and harmony, with the blessings to express your multidimensional creative abilities to be of service, my heartfelt desire is that this compilation gently guides you to that experience. It is liberating the soul, to explore its multidimensionality and to experience love. It is experiencing God.

This work reflects a personal spiritual journey, a search for an experience of God, offering a multidimensional analysis, a renewed awareness of what is most commonly described as the light and the darkness—reaching multiple aspects of life.

As you read this book, please contemplate every sentence thoughtfully and calmly. Experience the vibrational synergies of the words. They activate an energetic shift leading to evermore honor your beautiful beingness as well as all of life. Reading this book slowly in a contemplative way moves you through doorways of light, inviting blissful loving synergies within a creative space. Awareness is awakened from within.

The teachings and insights within this book are intended to guide you, and guide us all to step out from the illusory turmoil of the physical world—to live and breathe in true consciousness of the sanctity of life.

I am presenting ways to awaken within, a consciousness of the "sacred" toward all life, an oasis of pure love intrinsically embodied within all beings. Living within a consciousness of the sacred, naturally brings forth well-being as well as divine creativity expressed in all aspects of life.

Occasionally, I repeat ideas and words to associate them with different issues and aspects of life. This emphasis is to better guide you toward a place of serenity and bliss where true consciousness of the heart is awakened.

Throughout the book, I focus on twelve main aspects of life and God's divine qualities of love, in furtherance of a soul consciousness awakening—inviting peace on Earth. I explore the multidimensionality of life navigating through multiple aspects of life, synergistically inviting the expression of God's qualities—the twelve aspects of God.

I invite you to embrace with ease and grace all these qualities of love, God's blessings, guiding all beings to live in consciousness of their true divine nature—awakening the heart consciousness of the soul, the heart of the Tree of Life. Peace becomes then a living reality between all beings and all nations.

In the first aspect, surrendering brings about trust, allowing, creating, and manifesting in love and joy. I present guidelines, insights, and meditations to embrace God's qualities, the love light sourcing from all life—to surrender to the love and light sourcing from all life and to bask in that divine energy. It is my intent to lead you to experience the process of trusting life, allowing, creating, and choosing love. Surrendering is liberating. It is the path to an experience of your true identity, your sacredness, and the sacredness in all of creation. It is allowing Father-Mother God, the Creator, the highest power of love, divine consciousness, to be revealed in the "nowness" of every moment.

In the second aspect, I introduce guidelines to empower your prayers and meditations—and their importance in the process of surrendering. Praying is expressing and discovering the mystical and sacred aspect of your being and life—from the heart of your soul to the heart of creation—the supreme heart of God. Praying is learning to express your heart—the heart of your soul. Meditating is living a communion with and within the heart of the soul. It is a communion with the one heart of God. It is a communion of love. Throughout the book, I explain the beneficial aspects and blessings of living from the unified heart.

In the third aspect, it is important to recognize and connect with the consciousness of the physical body—and know how to listen to your whole body. I introduce insights about the harmonic power of conscious breathing. Living in consciousness of the breath leads to true consciousness, good health, balance, and joy. Throughout the book, I introduce guidelines to experience and sustain harmonious physical-emotional-spiritual synergy.

In the fourth aspect, I present insights to become free from guilt, blame, jealousy, animosity, judgment, and resentment—to choose love—always wishing love, joy, wellness, and goodness to every being. In the process of surrendering, I emphasize how important it is to become free from recurring fears, painful negative feelings and issues—to step out from a negative matrix with love, and embrace one's God-Self, i.e., your Higher Self.

The fifth aspect explores the bliss of forgiving and compassion. Surrendering is forgiving. Forgiving leads to boundless bliss, serenity, wellness, goodness, joy, and love consciousness. It opens the sacred space of your heart and leads to the portal of your God-Self. Surrendering and forgiving opens the heart to infinite compassion and nurturing love. Compassion is being free from all judgment. It is a state of awareness, forgiveness, and understanding that is nurturing and infinitely loving.

The sixth aspect introduces the magnetic power of gratitude. Gratitude opens the heart and empowers the mind through the heart. A consciousness of appreciation and gratitude is nurturing, loving, and tremendously empowering. It is a magnetic energy that unfolds goodness, wellness, and wholeness. In gratitude we create a world of fullness and abundance since we rejoice in all the blessings of life.

In the seventh aspect, I explore the power inherent in our feelings, emotions, intentions, thoughts, beliefs, and words. Responding to life with a consciousness of love, reverence, and joy comes from inner awareness.

It is possible to change the nature of our intentions, beliefs, and cellular programs to be living forces of goodness, compassion, and love the moment we truly connect with the essence of our being. The quality and nature of our intentions are leading creative forces.

I emphasize the power our choice of words has upon our lives. I explain how to expand unlimited potential in joy, wishing goodness to all beings and all of life. When we truly love one another, we exude light, activating and inviting goodness for all beings.

In the eighth aspect, through many facets of life, I lead you to a discovery and an understanding of your true nature, essence, and holiness—so that through such realization fears are transmuted into love. Embracing the realization of our quintessence is living from the heart, always walking on a path of faith and reverence. It is an awakening to a consciousness of the sacred and of honoring all beings and all of life. It is awakening to the heart's desire to be of service, to make a difference, to give and receive with love and in love.

The ninth aspect leads us to discover the realm of Mother Earth, the realm of the animals, and our sacred connection with nature's divine energies and intelligence. Embracing the sacredness in all life is living with consciousness, connecting with the multidimensionality of our being—God's consciousness, i.e., nature's consciousness.
The global energetic geometrical light grid holds all the divine codes of life—intelligent light patterns and design. It holds all sacred geometry of light from which all life is sourcing—from the heart and mind of God or God's consciousness.

In the tenth aspect, I explore the physical world and the spirit world—the visible and the invisible. I address our relationship with the physical world and the spirit world, how to live in harmonic synergy in both worlds, and how they both work and interact in absolute oneness. All that is visible, as matter, is emerging and manifesting from the invisible as pure energy frequencies. Navigating with consciousness within both worlds leads to a path of wellness and an understanding that there is no separation between the outer world and the inner world. All is unified.

The eleventh aspect presents insights about the light and the darkness—personal and global transcendence, dualism, and oneness. I introduce multiple views about what is called the light and the darkness. I present a personal outlook about a world of duality, how it is possible to step out from this dualism and awaken to one consciousness of love and reverence through the heart, to embrace Heaven on Earth, unity consciousness, and oneness.

The twelfth aspect reveals the experience of boundless divine creativity through the discovery of your purpose and mission—honoring your God-given gifts in service. Learning how to use your creative expression and abilities from the heart brings forth increasing wisdom, reverence, joy, and harmony. When qualities of love are awakened from within, it is possible to embrace an understanding of your purpose and mission.

It is a time of devotion. Devotion is about deep love, dedication, and perseverance. It is developing one's willingness in daily spiritual work, meditation, and in service to others and to the Earth Being. With daily spiritual work and service, you thrive as a living force of love, excelling in divine creativity, and expanding as a being of light.

These twelve main aspects are interrelated since one supports the other—and each includes additional related aspects.

In summary, this compilation supports the shift of the Tree of Life, activated and rebalanced within its new polarities for all humans to awaken to the supreme light sourcing from the heart—to experience unity consciousness. Opening the heart invites the light body to exude its luminescence.

This book takes you on a journey within the consciousness of your true divine identity in sacred ways, immersing in the heart of hearts and of your divine presence. The heart of hearts is the heart of God. This work is guiding you to discover and explore higher levels of consciousness—you are awakening right now.

Throughout my life, I have come to experience that embracing an awareness of these fundamental aspects of living from the heart activates an awakening of our light and an awareness of boundless divine creativity.

From that place of awareness, it is possible to explore the wonders of life—to be of service in harmony as a living force of love, a radiant sun. Living within this fundamental consciousness leads to an awakening of timeless dimensional light realities and miracles occur.

Such a path evolves toward an understanding of our relationships with the physical world and the spirit world—and our connection with nature's intelligence to ultimately embrace with joy and reverence all the sacredness of life.

I am inviting you on a path of discovery where the personality is gently transcended with love so that the soul is free to express its infinite beauty and divine qualities. It is the rebirth of the personality in its purest form and emanation. It is a place where the mind recognizes the qualities of the heart, immersing deeper and deeper within its consciousness of boundless unconditional love.

This creative work is easily accessible to people from all faiths, beliefs, nations, and worlds. To speak to "God" and of "God," please use the name/s you feel connected with. In your heart and soul, it will be the right name for you. God is omnipresent, omnipotent, omniscient, and expressed in infinite aspects and names such as Divine Consciousness, The Creator, Source, Divine Presence, or Love Life Force—sempiternal and unconditional, inherently at the source and light of All That Is.

ARTWORK RELATED TO THIS BOOK:

These twelve main aspects of God and doorways are in energetic resonance and oneness with the twelve artistic images I created—representing the sacredness of the Tree of Life—in my second book, *Twelve Doorways of Light: Sacredness of Life.*
Each image holds a vortex, a divine design of light, transmitting specific qualities of God. United, they support an activation of the Tree of Life—an experience of the divine living presence within us and in all life. These "doorways of light" sustain a sacred global space throughout our present ascension, contributing to the anchoring of the supreme divine light upon the earth plane, within all of life, bridging Heaven and Earth.
Each image brings forth an energetic support toward a greater ability to awaken and embrace one's holiness. Together they represent a Stargate of light, a holy pathway to experience the heart of God.

This artistic work is in harmonic synergy with the written messages presented in this book, supporting one another positively and creatively. It is a spiritual, contemplative, meditative transmission, adapted for today's global transcendence. It is a pathway to freedom, a new life, a new you, and a new world. (In chapter ten, you may read additional information about this artwork).

ADDITIONAL SUPPORT:

I invite you to view on my website artfromthelight.com images related to the Tree of Life and additional artistic expressions of peace love light frequency, uplifting, harmonizing, and energizing. My website offers resources and information related to this book, describing my professional services and life's purpose.

I have received from divine guidance a healing modality I have named "Synergism into Love". This is a powerful energy work, where Father Mother God, peace love light, ascended masters and archangels work through me and with me. To help my clients I hold clear loving intentions, prayers, positive visualization, and sometimes proceed with hands on healing—I clear my mind and commune with a holy space in my heart to receive divine guidance and let God.

For many years, I have practiced another very special healing modality that I would like to share with you.
Ellen Kaufman Dosick who has brought forth "The Soul Memory Discovery Work" or SMD from divine guidance describes it as follows:

> *"Soul Memory Discovery is a spiritual healing modality that enables you to access, identify, and release troubling issues that limit your lives and inhibit the full expression of your essence and your beings. Just as our bodies hold memories of everything that has happened for us in this lifetime, so our energy fields hold memories of everything that has ever happened for our souls. Through SMD, we are able to access all of those memories, and so, find the origins of any issue, be it*

emotional, physical, spiritual, relationship issues, addictions,
life patterns, etc. A very gentle, simple and easy process lifts
those origins out of your system, and once the symptoms are
no longer being sourced, they dry up and go away—leaving
us free to be everything that we came here to be!"

Ellen's spiritual teachings have changed my life forever in the most beautiful ways. To become a certified SMD Practitioner, Ellen teaches this healing modality a couple of times per year. To learn more about the classes, please visit Ellen's website: www.soulmemorydiscovery.com On Ellen's website you shall find a worldwide listing of Soul Memory Discovery Practitioners. In addition of helping people, some practitioners offer healing modalities and guidance to animals. Practitioners work in person or remotely since love light energy knows only oneness.

Based upon the Soul Memory Discovery work, the teachings of Ellen Kaufman Dosick—as well as my personal experience—it is important to first make sure that nothing is blocking light for the person. In SMD, it is called a "field clearing". This allows the person to open up to increasing awareness of his or her true being, the essence of life, and to experience a direct connection with Source/God. The person is then completely free in his or her own space. When there is nothing blocking light, all additional energies and issues that are not a match to "peace love light" come forth with greater clarity to be released and harmonized with ease, through love and in love.

The healing modalities I am presenting and practice are beautiful, gentle energy work. They are liberating, moving your beingness at such depth that they reprogram the memory of your cells. They take you to a place of surrendering and serenity, so that you may move into higher dimensions of light and greater consciousness of your divine purpose, mission, and awareness of your divine creative gifts.
Additionally, I teach "SMD" and "Synergism into Love" for personal self-empowerment and well-being.

Through prayers, willingness, spiritual work, faith, conscious breathing, and meditation you are learning to let go of painful issues. You are awakening the heart. A divine synergy of love is gently guiding you to an experience of your true and divine Self.

ACKNOWLEDGMENTS

I hereby convey heartfelt appreciation to all souls-spirits who have crossed my path, enriched my life, and contributed to this compilation.

Thank you to my spirit guides, angels of light, archangels, and masters of light who have been on my side through God's divine guidance and love.

I am so grateful to both my sisters, for being blessings in my life. Thank you for being a part of this divine work, supporting its journey into the world.

From my heart, special thanks to my dear friend attorney John Khoury, for his invaluable encouragement and support.

Thank you Jean Byrne, for your caring support and guidance when I began writing this book.

Oprah, you have inspired my life in boundless ways. It is because of you that I know that everything is possible. Thank you for shining your light into the world and for your countless gifts of love to all beings!

My heart holds infinite appreciation for all my animal friends who have taught me so much about the power of love and joy. They have opened my heart, teaching me unconditional love and oneness with nature's intelligence, their realm of existence, and with all of creation.

When creating this compilation, my primary incentive originated from my experience working with people and animals as a spiritual practitioner, and all the gifts emanating from these experiences through God's Divine Guidance. You have been my teachers and that continues to this day. This compilation is born from these experiences.

My heart is filled with reverence and humility to have been guided to convey these messages in words and through pictographic art, a gift from life I have the blessings and joy to pass on.

INTRODUCTION

My soul's purpose is to bring together all beings in love through the multiple creative expressions life has gifted me with, honoring and embracing a consciousness of the sacred.

I place the full expression of my being in God's loving care, inviting holy consciousness to lead my way and forever surrendering to where that path of service guides me.

This book is designed to support an awakening of our light bodies from the heart—awakening to divine cosmic consciousness, an experience of the one heart and mind of God or God's consciousness—inviting divine creativity and divine co-creative partnership in furtherance of peace and harmony for all beings.

If we do not resist this shift and awakening, we experience unity consciousness. Every human being has to do his or her part to choose and invite a resonance that is of God's divine qualities of love—of the Tree of Life—of the supreme heart and mind of God.

In the following segments, I would like to share with you the path that ultimately has drawn me to create *Twelve Doorways of Light: A Portal to your God-Self*.

It has always been my passion to be creative. As a child I loved drawing and painting, as well as reading and writing. They represented ways to escape from my daily environment. Being creative with words, colors, and forms was nurturing and comforting. I felt safe moving through the multidimensional infinite space of creativity, which was magical to me. Furthermore, the times spending in nature discovering the beauty of our world were the most beautiful and nurturing moments of my childhood. These moments were helping me to escape momentarily the pain and aloneness I was experiencing.

Throughout my childhood, my whole consciousness moved into a place of pain and confusion, leaving me feeling desperately lost, unloved, and abandoned. I was forgetting who I was. As I was growing up, this state was so painful that all life was hurting. This condition created a significant void within me, an endless feeling of dying into oblivion.

To the best of my ability, I was learning to abide by the adult's rules with all the sociological indoctrinations in order to hide so much of who I was and to look all right on the surface.

I could not understand what I was doing in my physical body. I felt dysfunctional, limited, and trapped in the wrong world, as if a part of my being was missing. I began a thorough search for that missing part, wishing to return to my source and understand who I am.

I began an unrelenting search for the freedom of my soul.
I searched to discover the most sacred aspect of my being, an opening door to the light and an experience of God—a pathway to "home". I began practicing meditation, yoga, and energy healing work to discover infinite dimensions of life.

As a child, I always had the desire to create harmony, peace, and loving energies within my surrounding and between people. I wished to understand the purpose of life.

With time, I understood that I had to learn how to bring forth, from within me, the true expression of my being, and convey the highest qualities of love, such as forgiveness, compassion, grace, joy, reverence, and divine creativity.

I understood that I had to cross the veil of illusion within the realm of physicality in order to see truth—to discover and experience my true Self, excelling in divine creativity and service and embracing life with joy.

With time I realized that life was, and is, endlessly leading me back to a consciousness of my God-Self, so that I may learn to serve all life in love and awareness, expressing infinite compassion. I came to an understanding that such opportunity is given to all human beings since we originate from the same divine design.

My teachers taught me ways to feel, see, direct, and transform energies to harmonize and bring forth the sacred energies and frequencies of love intrinsic to all life. From deep within my soul, I was reawakening divine ancient knowledge, a consciousness of the sacred, and of the love life force. I was rediscovering a consciousness of my true identity. This journey of discovery has never ended.

Ever since my early twenties I have been studying and experiencing diverse healing modalities to harmonize and balance the body, mind, and spirit, awakening to a consciousness of my God-given gifts—to raise consciousness about the indwelling and sacred attributes of life. My intention has always been to use these holy energies through God's divine guidance to serve the highest good in all life.

These healing modalities consist of energy work, hands-on healing, spiritual clearing, spiritual counseling, and cellular reprogramming, on site clearing and blessings, and earthbound spirit release. My deep love for animals has guided me to apply harmonizing modalities on them too.
From these teachings and my experience working with light and within God's light, as a spiritual practitioner, I have naturally intuitively

expanded further diverse ways of rebalancing energies to reach all levels of life—through God's divine guidance, working with the angels of light and archangels, and masters of light.

These experiences have been gifts of joy from life, inspiring the birthing of this compilation with my second book and its unique creative approach.

My path and inner search have granted me with the blessing to bestow twelve creative "doorways of light" reflected in an artistic symbolic expression, supporting individual and global divine transcendence. This artistic representation epitomizes the essence of this book. This artwork is available on my website and in my book, *Twelve Doorways of Light: Sacredness of Life*.

I intend by this book to demonstrate how it is possible to live in harmony in the midst of today's events and energies. I further intend to offer guidelines and solutions to awaken our greatest creative potential in order to live a blissful, meaningful life, and to build a peaceful world together.

As a new era is unfolding, a new consciousness of unity is awakening. All illusions of dualities are, with time, fading away, allowing the one consciousness of the heart to be revealed and to be recognized as the leading force—the power of love. My wish is that this compilation inspires readers to be seekers of their true identity, choosing a consciousness of the heart as a leading force of love.

As we are impelled to embrace increasing light, everything that does not match that light comes forth for healing. It is a global shift, a synchronized transmutation and an awakening. I have chosen to contribute to that awakening of the heart, by sustaining a consciousness of the sacred and pure love for all life—in the best of my ability. It is my joy, mission, and purpose—and it is your purpose!

We are brothers and sisters walking as one in the freedom of the light and

I love you. I am inviting you to play in the light and shine to love all beings and revere all life.

I will always be considerably honored and blessed to play in this world with all the beings of light I am to do great work with. Thank you for joining me on that journey of love and in love, of peace and in peace.

Sarah Jeane

Once upon a time I fell in love with life … and this is the gift.

A JOURNEY INTO THE LIGHT:

I was enjoying an afternoon of painting (a painting about divine Mother Earth), feeling blissful and serene, when I suddenly felt very tired. I decided to lie on the couch and close my eyes to pray and meditate for a short time. In my meditation, I suddenly consciously felt that I was leaving my physical body. I was being divinely guided by gentle, loving Presences.

I arrived in a meadow. Trees and bushes were nearby. I moved closer to one very large bush and then moved around it. I was moving in the air. I found myself in the presence of a luminescent, radiant light being. Infinite, unconditional love emanated from him as well as an incredible bright light. He was tall and muscular. His skin was a magnificent shade of gold. One shoulder was partially covered by a robe falling graciously around his harmoniously shaped body. His robe was almost the same color as his skin. His facial features appeared to be Asian. The radiant luminescent light and the unconditional love emanating from this being seemed to emerge from all of life, endlessly embracing all of creation and myself completely—as two huge, radiant white wings were holding me so gently, so lovingly.

I was held and embraced by perfect, incredible, pure love light energy. I was experiencing an amazing ecstatic place of bliss and love, bathing in the most luminous white light. My whole being was light love energy consciousness. I became a ray of light and of love energy. I was experiencing

1

my true essence. I was living the consciousness of the heart of my soul. It was oneness, pure love consciousness—God consciousness. I was one light within all light. In that light, I was experiencing pure perfect ecstatic love consciousness, and nothing of a lesser energy was coming through. I wanted to stay in this place of pure love consciousness forever.

I was held in that love and luminous light for a long time, though I am not sure how long. All of a sudden, I was moving at a very high speed toward the sky and the cosmos among the stars and galaxies. It was spectacular, amazingly delightful, and blissful. I felt so loved and protected.

I was moving among the stars. My consciousness was expanding and expanding in infinite ways. I was experiencing limitless time and space, a divine consciousness of my soul, of my whole being in infinity. It was an ecstatic experience of oneness. When I came back to my physical body, I was in the same position on the couch. I remained still for a long time, my eyes closed, wanting to hold on to the experience of that perfect pure love light energy and frequency—acknowledging in reverence and bliss the presence of this incredible being of light.

My physical body felt light, and my mind was blissfully serene. Even back in my physical body, my whole beingness was sustained in the embrace of that pure love and light energy. I was aware of a bright light emanating from me, and it was present all around me. I wanted to maintain within my beingness the blissful feeling of the purest experience of love and oneness. Later, I understood that this light being is one of my master guides. I named him "Angelic Master of Light" because his incredible bright light embraced me as two loving wings holding me so gently.

That love light energy was an experience of oneness encompassing all beings and all of creation. It was pure love consciousness and perfection.

In my heart, I expressed endless gratitude for receiving the gift of that experience—and I still do. The experience changed my life forever. I received a clear understanding and experience of my essence, of the love light energy embodied within me and within all beings and all life. I experienced oneness

as a blissful place of unconditional love for all life, from the deepest place in my heart. No being is alone or separated from God and creation. We are God's light consciousness, endlessly receiving divine guidance and bliss from that same eternal source of divine love consciousness emerging from our hearts and the heart of all life. Our guides of the light, angels, and archangels are eager to assist us as guardians, guides, and messengers.
They naturally hold a consciousness of the Divine Living Presence.

I experienced the heart of God within and without, in me and in all that is, a state of serene perfection, wholeness, holiness, and sacredness.
*I understood that "**we and God are one**".*

I am a ray of light emanating from the radiance of God.

Within every being are inherently embedded infinite possibilities and the divine living presence of God, of love, since all life is sourcing from the same Divine Design, as a flow of sempiternal love.

CHAPTER ONE

Surrendering Brings about Trust, Allowing, Creating, and Manifesting in Joy

B EFORE READING THIS BOOK FURTHER, please place your hands on your heart chakra anahata, located in the middle of your chest at the same level that your physical heart. Close your eyes and breathe peace love light in your heart chakra anahata to activate the sound of the "celestial realm." This is what "anahata" means in Sanskrit. Practice until you feel a warm energy of love awakening.

Then place your hands on your sacred heart. It is your high heart chakra. The sacred heart is located just above your heart chakra anahata at the level of the thymus in the center of your upper chest. Breathe peace love light. Practice until your feel love energy activating. You will feel warm, nurturing, and loving energies moving in these centers.

> *I ask that my heart chakra anahata be now unified with my sacred heart in divine love. I breathe in the love of God. I choose to live within the consciousness of the heart of my soul, now and forever. Living in the heart of my soul is living in the oneness of the heart of all hearts—the heart of God. My soul is the pure expression of my God-Self. It is the energetic emanation of my spiritual essence. God's divine*

light is embracing me, living in me, nurturing me, and showering me with boundless gifts of love.

Breathe in the energy of that divine union and oneness. This union awakens and activates the heart of your divine essence or soul. You are experiencing the one heart of unity consciousness, living within you. It is the portal to your God-Self—a place where you experience the supreme heart of God. This book is supporting this journey of the heart to your God-Self.

Practice this prayer and meditation any time you wish to be uplifted, when you wish to open your heart to experience and feel unconditional love—unity consciousness and connect with your God-Self. It can be for example while gazing at a sunrise or sunset. It is a spiritual experience permeating your whole beingness and expanding to all life and creation. Your heart is a sun shinning its rays to touch all beings and all life in divine ways.

Breathe with consciousness the love and beauty emanating from all creation and from within you. Learn to awaken warm feelings of love sourcing from your heart, allowing its natural vibrations to nurture you and to nurture all life.
Living the one consciousness of the heart activates a supreme light and awakens the light body to awakening you!

Choose love, always, and learn to be present in the consciousness of the one unified heart.

In the book, every time I mention the heart, I am referring to the unified sacred heart consciousness.

I open my heart, allowing divine love consciousness to flow boundlessly now and always. I breathe in joy, the love sourcing from all that is. It is in the choice of oneness, of unconditional love awakened from the heart that I shall be blessed in infinite ways and awakened to all of who "I Am".

With time, you learn and know how to live every moment of your life from the heart of your soul, loving you, loving all beings, and loving life.

The heart of your soul is of Divine Consciousness also called Christ Consciousness or Buddhic Consciousness or Cosmic Consciousness or God's Consciousness. You are programmed with pure unconditional love consciousness. Choose to express your true essence now!

> *As I am surrendering, I choose to be anchored with love in the consciousness of the essence of my being, so that all that I am is revealed to me, now and always.*

> *As I am surrendering, I breathe in the stillness of my inner being, inviting divine love consciousness to guide my path and to be blessed by God's light.*

> *As I am surrendering, my relationship with God becomes a living reality.*

> *I live and breathe in the consciousness of my God-Self. All that I am is everlastingly revealed to me, now and always.*

> ***I navigate with ease within the consciousness of my inner sacred being, living a consciousness of love, of the sacred—of God.***

Surrendering awakens the ability to trust, allow, create and manifest through love. It allows you to create from your heart and from a consciousness of God—you are learning to see and acknowledge all the blessings of life, which is the ultimate path to happiness.

Surrendering is a process and a path leading to the discovery of your truth, your true essence. The true power of love is expressed from within. Live within that truth and touch people's lives with a magic wand of love and infinite blessings.

Surrendering is moving from the belief of not having and separation to an awareness of wholeness and oneness with all of creation. It is stepping into the realization of your ultimate divine union with Source. It is learning to trust life. It is stepping into the realization and experience that life is being supportive and that all you need to do is to accept receiving love in love. Surrendering leads to a place of grace, bliss, and freedom.

Grace is a quality of the heart. Grace is of love, honoring, compassion, true consciousness, bliss, and beauty. Grace is the voice of your God-Self. Grace is an emanation sourcing from the beauty of the soul. Grace is a gentle loving whisper from the angels.
There is grace beneath all forms and expressions of life.

When you surrender, you experience grace and live in grace.

WE ARE COSMIC BEINGS

Many people feel that they are not from this planet. If you feel that you are not from this world, it is likely that your "soul birth" has originally not taken place on Earth. Earth is much younger (about 4.6 billion years) then the universe is (about sixteen billion years or more). In reality, you are seeded and coded with the memory-knowledge of many other cosmic beings.

Walking in your present physical form, you have chosen to experience the true consciousness of your being, transcending the physical and all human thought forms. You are expanding your consciousness in divine ways by being of service through your mission and purpose—living and working in synergy with the Earth Being and all of life (Earth is a living breathing being with consciousness). It is a spiritual occurrence since you are a spiritual being—a divine soul temporarily navigating in the company of a physical form. Your physical form is a sacred vehicle intended for divine purpose.

Most people are familiar with the seven-chakra system and the seven bodies, but since your DNA/RNA and your whole beingness are infused with higher frequencies, you are activating additional energy centers/chakras and bodies of light consciousness within your beingness. Your spiritual Self, your light body, is awakening. This work is guiding you to discover and explore higher levels of consciousness—you are awakening right now.

Supreme light is activated in the heart when you choose to live in harmonic synergy with the consciousness of your God-Self, which is your true Self. All qualities of love are expressed through the personality. This supreme light activates all your energy centers and all of your bodies of light.
Your heart is holding your sacred code, your holy name, and your signature. It is a holy sound frequency unique to you. Beings from higher dimensions of light communicate through that unique frequency of the heart. We can do the same as we activate our unified heart. Globally, we are returning to our true sources. We are discovering our multidimensionality and oneness of the heart.

We are globally moving toward unity consciousness of the heart. Our oneness and divine Self are progressively revealed and experienced. The Tree of Life encompassing our divine design is activated from within in its wholeness. We are awakening.

I open my heart and choose to be a source of boundless love and compassion. I rejoice in the warm radiance of my heart and divinity. My vibrational frequency rises to high frequencies of divine love, unfolding and expanding unlimitedly. I experience the unconditional love of God emanating from my heart, my whole being, and from all life.

The Ancient Ones (the Mayans, the Hindus, the Egyptians, and the Hopis) speak of the beginning of a new age where the "consciousness of the heart" is revealed and awakened. They speak of a new paradigm and the end of an age. They speak of the beginning of a new age—a new era—a Golden Age where we are globally awakening to experiencing true consciousness; love light consciousness. They speak of a global transition from the third to the fourth and to the fifth dimension. During that transition, all that is not of love and reverence within the density of the physical world—and from all levels of life—comes forth for release and transmutation, allowing a new energetic harmonic alignment to take place—to ultimately merge in synergy with the light of the fifth dimension.

During that transition, we are awakened to our true essence, holding the desire for love and reverence. We are uplifted and showered with infinite blessings of love consciousness. It is said that we are assisted by divine beings from the Galactic Federation of Light. We are assisted by ascended masters, archangels, multiple light beings and angels, and that we are encoded to awakening to our God-Self.

The messages in this book support and guide you to recognize, allow, liberate, and embrace all of your sacred gifts and inner beauty as we enter a new paradigm of higher dimensions of light.

As the new Earth is emerging, we are awakening to a consciousness of love, of God—the hearts are uniting and the one sacred heart is awakening. It is the union of Heaven and Earth. This divine union brings forth peace on Earth, the Garden of Eden upon the Earth Being, into our hearts, and in all of life.

It is a time to lovingly transcend the world of physicality and allow the multidimensionality of our beingness to be revealed. The world of physicality is uplifted to higher frequencies of light consciousness and expands in unity with the spirit world. All life unifies in the oneness of the supreme light, a consciousness of the heart as one force of pure love consciousness. **This book is designed to further a journey of the heart.**

As cosmic beings and beings of God, we are multidimensional and coded with incredible divine knowledge, wisdom, and gifts. We are coded and one with God's infinite qualities—holy love light consciousness—embedded in the Tree of Life and the Flower of Life. When the radiance of your light is revealed, it liberates your God-given gifts in multidimensional creative ways.

Choose to awaken divine qualities from within, unique gifts, unlimited creativities, and potentialities in service to all life.

My wish is that these insights and this creative work open your heart to embrace all life in loving-kindness, so that you may open doorways of joy and bliss wherever you may be, since this is what this work has done for me.

WHEN THE POWER OF PRAYER AND MEDITATION BECOMES THE POWER OF LOVE

Praying/meditating is surrendering to the highest power of love. Praying/meditating is adjusting and shifting your frequency, learning to emanate love consciousness, and experiencing the true nature of the soul. It is opening the heart to know true love and bliss, in the still voice of your being.

Praying/meditating is connecting with the heart. Praying is an energetic alignment preparing you for meditation.

Praying is the process of being fully conscious in the moment, present within the holiness of your inner being, from which place you talk to God—it is a holy communion. Praying is a vibrational frequency of love and joy emanating from within your heart and from your presence. From that place, you have the ability to touch people's hearts. You are opening doorways of light for all life to embrace.

Throughout the book, I go into greater details about these doorways so that you may empower your prayers and meditations with the highest frequency of love. This journey guides you to surrender and to be a blessing to all life.

Praying is about experiencing true consciousness in the presence of every moment and acting accordingly within that truth in service of all life.

When you pray, open your heart and mind to the vastness of all possibilities and know that you are never walking alone. In reality, you have the innate ability and choice to embrace loving boundless support sourcing from the intrinsic presence of God within you, within all life—encompassing all of creation.

You are walking in oneness within the consciousness of a divine cosmic grid of love light among loving and divine presences assisting you. Divine guides of light, master guides, angels of light, archangels, ascended masters, and nature's intelligence are eager to assist you within God's love light. You have free will to embrace their loving presence and support. Invite them in your prayers and meditations and communicate with them from your heart. Listen to their messages—you will receive divine teachings, guidance, and unconditional love and gifts.

Your guardian angels, master guides of light, archangels, ascended masters, and nature's intelligence are eager to assist you, as you open your heart to a divine creative power. It is a cosmic power of love, God's infinite divine qualities within you and expressed in all life. Within God's peace love light consciousness—in your prayers—you may call upon their love and divine assistance. Many light beings are assisting you within God's consciousness of unconditional love.

Listen to the voice of the heart. It is a place of inner stillness. It is the voice of love. In that stillness, you have the ability to experience the divine frequency and emanation of your being, of all life, and of the supreme heart of God. You are in meditation.

From that stillness, you are discovering a new and infinite realm of boundless love. From that stillness, you are receptive to infinite emanations of love. From the divine emanation of your being flows true sacred knowledge with all the beauty of your soul's gifts.

Experience your breath as a flow of love light force, nurturing you and loving you. As you become conscious of your breathing, gently free your mind from all thought forms. Breathe in your heart. Pay attention to the energetic loving emanation of your heart. Then pay attention to the divine love energy emanating from all forms of life. Practice!

Praying is expressing and discovering the mystical and sacred aspect of your being and life—from the heart of your soul to the heart of creation, the one heart of God. Praying is learning to express the heart of your God-Self.

In your prayers, look for all the gifts of life and for all you have been taking for granted—and express gratitude. Gratitude opens your heart and connects you with the fullness and abundance of life in nurturing and joyous ways. Feelings of gratefulness in your prayers bring you to create more of what you are grateful for. Gratefulness holds powerful magnetic frequencies of unity, reverence, and love. It is an energetic flow of fullness, abundance, wholeness, and oneness.

When you are surrendering, you are learning to live in true consciousness of your power—the power of love. Praying is surrendering. Praying is revering life. Praying is saying, *thank you*. Praying is leading you to a communion with Spirit—with God.

Meditating is living a communion with God within the heart of the soul. It is a communion with the consciousness of God. It is a communion of love.

Praying/meditating is getting in touch with your essence and heart's deepest desires. It is connecting deep within—with the sacredness of your being and the sacredness of all that is in creation. It is living your oneness with God. Praying is softening the ego with love and allowing true consciousness to be revealed. It is opening your heart to love. It is opening your heart to your divine gifts and unlimited creativity. Slowly, lead your prayer into meditation. Explore your multidimensionality from the deepest emanation of your being; your heart sings.

> *I anchor my consciousness in my heart and in the sempiternal love and beauty of God's divine presence.*
> *My divine essence is my God-Self. In my prayers and meditations, I discover the power of the love emanating from my God-Self, where I experience pure being—I*

experience the heart and mind of God—I experience pure
love consciousness.

In your prayers send peace love light and blessings to all beings and the world. Open your heart with infinite compassion and pray for people who need loving support and healing. Your prayers are received by all of life.

Praying is moving into a place of awareness, reverence, gratefulness, love, and serenity. It is opening to your heart's deepest desires and expressing them to God. Praying is learning to become free from illusory beliefs, leading to suffering and infringing upon the divine realization of your God-Self. Praying is choosing love, awareness, and harmony. It is learning about true consciousness.

Prayers are gently leading you to an awareness of your divine beingness. Praying activates a divine alignment with the mind, the personality, and the soul—preparing you for meditation.

Moving into true consciousness is becoming free from all resistance and global thought forms—the loving divine frequencies of your beingness and of all life are revealed. It is surrendering. Surrendering prepares you for meditation. Surrendering is praying.

I am a divine being radiating God's infinite qualities and
light. I radiate heavenly vibrant light colors and hues of joy
and beauty.

Place your hands on your heart center and breathe deeply in your whole body and field. Breathe in your heart the love and light of God. Feel the unconditional love. Find that place of stillness and wellness within you.

Contemplate all the goodness of your life and all the beauty of your world. Think about all the people you love. Fill your heart with gratitude. Visualize how you are smiling at one another. See the vibrant colors of a rainbow embracing you all. When you see the rainbow, invite in the rainbow the people you have resented. See all the people you have resented smiling at you. Breathe in the love of God deeply and gently. Witness the radiant color energies of the rainbow transmuting all negative feelings into love energies and qualities. Fill your heart center with compassion, appreciation, and joy.

As you release all negative feelings into the rainbow, the light transforms them into vibrations of compassion and love.

Becoming compassionate is becoming aware—it is forgiving. Compassion heals and opens all hearts. Being compassionate is receiving clarity and understanding. It is being free from all judgment. It is loving boundlessly. It is seeing, knowing, and experiencing the sacredness in all life. It is a place of complete awareness and unconditional love.

When you express compassion you become aware. This awareness naturally transforms all negative feelings and judgments into love.

Fill your heart with deep appreciation and gratitude. Open your heart to feelings of love and compassion. Learn to love unconditionally and learn to receive love with an open heart, infinite gratitude, and grace.

Knowing how to give with love is receiving. Knowing how to receive with love is giving. Experiencing love is opening the heart and allowing love to flow. It is experiencing the qualities of the heart. It is bliss!

When you experience deep love or the life light force, you are in a place of empowerment because good feelings engender additional good feelings and harmony. From such a place, you live in a sacred space. It is a nurturing space that you have built from within and discover. This nurturing space you have created is holding your prayers in honoring and sacredness.

Sacred space holds high energy of peace, love, light, and reverence. It supports and empowers the realization of your true essence, your purpose, your mission, and your heart's desires. It is a space of serenity where you are in direct contact with inner divine guidance, allowing divine consciousness to guide you and nurture you.

*As I surrender, I am learning to be conscious of my breathing.
I am learning to experience the life force in the movement of
my breathing. I am learning to listen to the still voice within.
I am learning to listen to the presence of God within. I am
learning to live in consciousness and with consciousness. I am
blessed and I am a blessing.*

*I live within the sacred space and flow of my breathing. I live
within the sacred space of my heart and of my soul.*

Creating sacred space is in reality an acknowledgment of the
sacredness and holiness encompassing every moment, within all space
and dimensions. It is a holy consciousness encompassing all beings, the
Earth Being with all of creation—it is a place of unconditional love
embedded within you.

It is possible to live within "sacred space" in every moment by responding
to life with wisdom, reverence, honoring, and gratitude, and by expressing
infinite compassion—always living from the heart. It is a consciousness
of love. A consciousness of the heart is of the sacred. From the heart,
you naturally embrace all of life with love and in love; you are living in
love. Living within sacred space is living with consciousness in every
present moment.

In your prayers and throughout this book, please choose the name/s
representing the idea of God, The Creator of All That Is, and Peace
Love Light consciousness. Feel good about the name/s you choose:
Lord, Divine Power, Divine Source, Father Mother God, The Creator,
The Great One, Creator of All That Is, Yahweh, Jehovah, Elohim, and
the like. The concept of Father Mother God's consciousness is divinely
expressed through many names, forever omnipresent, omniscient,
omnipotent, and intrinsic with the highest order of peace love light—as
the essence of life and from which all life springs.

Pray from your heart to activate a blissful flow of love and doorways
of light. These doorways of light are revealing the divine synergies of the
Tree of Life within you. The Tree of Life—activated in you—reveals

your light body and all qualities of God in action. Your wholeness and divinity are expressed. Pray within a consciousness of the sacred and love for all life. The Tree of Life within you holds the divine design of your God-Self.

The nature of your intention holds the vibration of what you create in the now. In the now you are creating your experience. It is creating what comes next, but you will always be in the now moment. In the now, you have power over your experience. Your thoughts, feelings, and intentions are energy frequencies received by all of creation. Since all is energy, creation responds to the frequencies you project and focus upon—in every moment of your life.

If you sustain a consciousness of the sacred and live within that consciousness, you invite divine creativity and divine knowledge to be expressed from the core of your being. It is an awakening. Your consciousness expands in light.

> It is from the core of my being, my heart, that the supreme light shines its rays. I embrace the vastness of my God-Self and magnificence in love.
>
> Lord, may your holy consciousness and supreme light be awakened in my heart! May I live the embodiment of your glory, of your love, so that I may serve the Earth Being with all its inhabitants in love!

Find this special space of stillness, bliss, and serenity within you. That space emerging from the heart is infinitely creating and creative. Exude that serene energy and bathe in that blissful space. From that blissful space in your heart express your prayers—then bring the mind back into stillness and meditate in the serenity of the heart.

Breathe deeply and slowly. Surrender and find a peaceful space within you.

> Father Mother God, please guide my whole being with my

*personality to serve from the holiness of my heart, in the light
that I am.*

I am a ray of light in the radiance of God.

Be still and bask in the emanation of your divine Self. It is the
emanation of the consciousness of God within you. Experience the love
of God emanating from all life permeating your whole beingness.

Praying is also dwelling on your heart's desires and infusing them
with God's love, joy, and harmony. It is allowing the process of divine
creativity to serve the highest purposes.

When you move from prayer into meditation and from meditation
into prayer, you are empowering your prayers and meditations with
energies of love and bliss. You are also empowering creative visions with
peace love light vibrations and frequencies.

Some teachers state that we cannot live without having desires.
Others say that we have to drop all our desires and expectations in order
to allow a divine creative flow of goodness, peace, and happiness.

If your visions and desires hold no negative feelings, if you express
peace, harmony, beauty, and reverence, you are in harmonic synergy
with all of life and with you!
In every moment we create from our state of consciousness, from our
perceptions, intentions, thought forms, feelings, and choice of words.
We create an experience according to the nature of the vibration we
emanate in every moment.

Because we are intrinsically infinitely creative beings and divine, we
have visions. If these visions are of high-frequency energy, they emanate
from a divine consciousness we have nurtured within. They support a
journey in harmony with all life. Learn to create from a place of blissful
serenity, reverence, awareness, sacredness, and joy, trusting the flow of
life. You then bask in God's love.

Since we are inherently creative beings, we emanate energy frequencies, express feelings, wishes, and dreams—we sometimes have expectations. Expectations often hold feelings of despair—watch out for this. As you surrender learn to trust the process of life. Invite and allow peace love light flow.

When expectations are expressed in painful feelings of despair, it is important to transcend these emotions by learning to trust and surrender. Give all to God. Invite and allow divine consciousness and the love of God to lead your path. Open your heart to all love!

In every moment, commune with the essence of your presence and its holiness so that your experience and dreams are devoid of any sense of exterior identification with form, thought, pain, or attachment—so that Spirit is free to work and create through you within a sacred infinite creative space. You are living an awareness of your true identity and sacredness.

> *I choose to emanate peace, reverence, and love. My divine presence is serene and infinitely loving. God's boundless qualities of love and light permeate my being.*

Focus on your breathing, and forget about any exterior circumstances. Gently let go of all thought forms. There is only love life force—it is you—breathing this force. Breathe peace love light in every part of your body slowly and deeply. Breathe peace love light in all your energy centers. Breathe peace love light in your body and field. Connect within and say: *Peace love light flows in me, through me, and in my life boundlessly, now and forever! It is an infinite flow of nurturing love and harmonic abundance and wealth. I am divine love and live in the love of God. I am the embodiment of peace, love, and light. I live in the supreme heart and mind of God. God lives in me.*

Repeat these words as a mantra any moment you wish to activate your light and bring forth a positive flow of energy—when you wish to uplift yourself. Experience within and without a flow of nurturing love. You are surrendering with ease. You are discovering your true identity. When you experience your true identity, you never identify with anything else or anyone else. You have an experience of you! You have an experience of the power of love and beauty of the divine Self.

When you move your attention inward and meditate, you develop a willingness to give and serve in holy ways. Your life's purpose becomes clear, and your heart longs to uplift and enrich others' lives in loving ways. The sacred cosmic forces of love are nurturing you and guiding you on your path. Your prayers are then energies inviting boundless love, wellness, abundance, and goodness for all beings and for you.

Your heart's desires, wishes, and dreams are transcended into a higher place where God's qualities are expressed, leading the way. It is a place of creative freedom. You are now living in true consciousness of your wholeness. From that place, all expectations—often leading to disappointment—are pointless and fade away in your consciousness since you have reached a new awareness of oneness and of the sacred presence within all of life. God's divine love and creative consciousness are revealed in your life—and in action. You are now aware that expectations have been limiting your human experience. In the freedom of your consciousness, you are inviting boundless creative energies to be expressed in holiness and in love.

My heart's desires, wishes, and dreams lead to divine visions manifesting with ease and grace—contributing to the highest good of life. This is where the shift occurs. This is the gift!

Wholeness is experienced when you are never again feeling disempowered by anything or anyone saying and doing—when you have surrendered and reconciled with "you" and life—when you live in blissful serenity and love consciousness—when you live in the consciousness of your divinity or true identity—when you enjoy being of service to others—when you express divine creativity and your God-given gifts—when you love "you", all beings, and all life.

Surrendering is learning to become whole. Surrendering is learning to trust the process of life. It is trusting that life is forever supporting your journey to wholeness. It is learning about faith and it is discovering your God-Self.

Feelings of joy hold a beautiful, sacred space. They are like prayers since they hold high vibrations that are liberating. *In joy, I surrender.* Joy, serenity, poise, love, beauty, bliss, grace, faith, trust, compassion, reverence, and gratefulness are qualities associated with surrendering. They empower the experience of your oneness and God-Self. Embrace them all and choose to live within the consciousness of these qualities. All these qualities are of the heart, revealed and lived in a state of surrendering.

In your sacred space, acknowledge the presence of God's peace love light and divine guidance. Invite in your space your divine master guides, the angels of light and archangels, who are assisting you and guiding you. You may call upon any of the ascended masters. They are eager to assist you on your journey into oneness and are holding your prayers and creative expressions in holiness. You are never alone.

Ascended masters, master guides, angels of light, and archangels are messengers of God and divine guides. They are messengers of light assisting you on your journey—with your life's work to serve all life. They are a conscious source and expression of God's love light divine qualities, offering divine guidance and unconditional loving support. You are not different. You are of God's love and light consciousness. Your prayers, spiritual work, and meditations are leading you to an experience of God. We are all from the same source of love.

Awaken to a consciousness of your oneness with light! Light is love consciousness.

When you are serene and have faith, you are experiencing a sense of oneness with all of creation. You are experiencing the essence of life. Faith empowers your prayers tremendously and empowers awareness.

SARAH JEANE

When you have faith, you are surrendering and experiencing harmonious energetic alignment with all life.

Faith brings forth a new space within your consciousness and beingness. Through faith, you are able to allow, create, manifest, give and receive with ease and grace. You are opening a space that is empowering. Learn to sustain that sacred space in love. This divine creative space encompasses infinite possibilities.

If you are not feeling well, if you wish to release heavy and unpleasant energies, call upon Father Mother God/Source/the Creator, divine guides and masters of light, archangels and angels of light to assist you and guide you.

> *Father Mother God, Divine Creator, dear Lord, please teach me to activate the full expression and consciousness of your holiness in my heart—guide me to experience and live in the consciousness of my true identity, the true nature of my essence.*
>
> *I choose to release into the light of God all energies that do not belong to me. God's love is forever expressed through me and within me. Father Mother God, thank you for activating the supreme light in me. I am the embodiment of your light. I am love consciousness—love is the presence of God within me.*

Pray from the consciousness of your unified heart. Connect within and become conscious of your breathing. Meditate and invite a blissful nurturing space—experience the holiness of your presence.

Do not judge any of your feelings and thoughts—just observe them as separated from you! You can then let them go and focus on the true emanation of your divine being.

> *I choose to be anchored in the consciousness of my divine Self. Truth is revealed to me. I choose to live right now in that consciousness of truth that is of pure love consciousness. I choose to breathe and live in the flow of love.*

22

I breathe in the blissful serene consciousness of my God-Self now and always.

Repeat the prayers several times until you are experiencing a relief, and the serenity of God's love within you. Boundless love energy is embracing you. Enjoy the love sourcing from the heart of your being and sourcing from the heart of all creation. Breathe and rest bathing in God's love consciousness.

Welcome any light color that is naturally embracing you. Meditate and bask in the light of God.

You may end your prayer bathing in the love of a very bright white-golden light or white-pink light, nurturing you. Or you might be guided to embrace the nurturing, loving, purifying energies of the violet light or purple light. Enjoy the love and light offered to you. Your mind is free from all thought forms.

Throughout your prayers hold a consciousness of gratefulness in your heart. Extend feelings of gratefulness all the way to the end of your prayers and in all aspects of your life.

Meditation: Express deep gratitude to Father Mother God, your guidance team, to Mother Earth, and to all life. Breathe deeply and slowly, peace love light in your heart. Breathe God's love. Experience the energy expanding and moving through you.

Then breathe peace love light deeply and slowly in the third eye—in the middle of your forehead. Direct your breathing from the middle of your forehead all the way to the middle of your brain. Breathe in your brain the peace love light of God. Then direct the breathing all the way to the top of your head.

From above your head, breathe peace love light throughout your whole body to your feet and under your feet—experience the energetic bond with the Earth Being under your feet for a little while. Then move the breathing throughout the whole body and back all the way above your head, breathing peace love light. Now move back in the heart. Breathe peace love light in the heart and direct your breathing in the palms of your hands. Experience the energy of God's love in the "heart" of your palms. Then breathe in your heart. Feel again your energetic connection with the Earth Being.

Breathe the love light of God in your heart and in your whole being and into the Earth. It anchors your prayers and the light in your whole being, your heart, and the Earth. Repeat this meditation three, seven, or twelve times. Breathe slowly, consciously, and deeply. Experience the energies of the words. Between every step, move into an inner silence within the breath and meditate. Meditate at the end of this process and express gratitude.

> *As my light awakens, I enjoy its infinite expansion. I am safe, bathing in God's peace, love, and light. I am safe and loved in the heart of God. Mother Earth nurtures me.*

You may proceed with this prayer and mediation in your space alone—or you may invite your friends and loved ones to participate.

Enjoy the divine blissful energies you have just welcomed in your space; this is another of the many ways to create a nurturing space, a sacred space where you feel serene, loved, and free. It is a space from where you nurture an energetic power to create and serve from a place of infinite love and faith. It is a place of complete surrendering.

With time, this inner state of blissful serenity becomes your way of life—a blissful force to create in divine ways and to serve all beings with love.

Surrendering is learning to love your Self. It is learning to love all beings and all creation. Surrendering is opening your heart to all qualities of God.
Praying and meditating lead you to that experience. It is an experience of who you are.

COLOR LIGHT

In your prayers—and any time you wish—you have the ability to invite light colors of the rainbow and work with these colors and any light color you wish. Every light color is associated with qualities of God, within you, also emanating frequencies in unity with life divine emanation. Colors emanate light frequencies and energies and you are light energy emanating a multitude of hues. It is purifying and uplifting to work with light colors. For example, the violet ray, the violet light, or violet flame purifies and transmutes all fears and negative issues into love light harmonic energies.

The golden ray or golden light illuminates the mind through the heart to bring clarity, serenity, and wisdom. It is possible to harmonize and energize your whole being (all your bodies and fields all the way to the core of the cells, DNA, and RNA) when working with colors and light frequency.

> *Father Mother God, master guides, divine guides of light, and archangels, please show me which light color ray or rays are benefiting me today to energize and strengthen my inner being, my mind, my spirit, all my bodies and fields, my cells, DNA, and RNA. Thank you.*

Breathe the light color ray(s) moving into your field, and infuse your whole being and space with the radiant color(s) for a few seconds or one minute. Let it move through you, entering the Earth.

You may ask in your prayers: *Please God, show me which light color rays are benefiting this event or situation to serve all of life's highest good.* From the sacredness of your heart within, allow and witness the light color(s) embracing the whole situation.

It is possible to proceed with the same prayers working with crystals' light colors. If you love crystals, it is possible to bring them into your space energetically or around any situation for support, harmonization, clearing, purification, healing, or energizing. They hold multiple clearing, energizing, and harmonizing qualities of love.

CLEARING AND HARMONIZING

Smudging your space with sage for a few minutes while you pray helps the clearing and harmonizing process. It is a nice support to hold the space in sacredness. In addition, you may display feathers (air), crystals (earth), a bowl of water (change the water once or twice a day), and light a candle (fire)—or keep a little light on. All these elements are nurturing purifying energies and are creating a sacred space to support the harmonizing process of your prayers.

Open your windows and allow light energy of the sun to enter and bathe your home with life force. If you build a home, it is extremely beneficial that the entrance of your home faces the sunrise. It infuses your home with life light force energy, which is beneficial to your well-being.

Keep your crystals clear. Smudge sage around them once in a while or run cool water over them. Ask that they be cleared from all foreign energies and that their highest sacred emanations of love, harmony, and light radiate naturally from the core of their beingness revealing their unique qualities. Express gratitude to receive these beautiful energies and gifts from your crystals. The sun and moon's energetic emanations are also very purifying and energizing—balancing yin and yang energies.

Bless your feathers, water, and candle lights. Ask for the highest energies of love, light, and harmony with all their sacred unique qualities to be revealed and emanate in all time, space, and dimensions.

Invite in your space your divine guidance team with reverence— within God's light. As you proceed with a clearing and harmonization of your home and property, ask for any energy frequency that is not of God's love consciousness to be released into the light of God and transmuted into love by God's light—in all four directions, above and below and all spaces in between. Pray audibly and clearly while you are smudging your home with sage. If possible, pray with a feather in holiness. Through this prayer, you are inviting balance, harmony, and light to be restored and revealed. Ask that all consciousness in that space be suffused with God's peace, love, light, joy, wellness, goodness, abundance, and harmony.

In your prayer, acknowledge one more time that your home, property, space, and crystals are infinitely blessed with God's peace, love, light, divine boundless qualities, and harmony through and from all six directions (all four directions, above and below), in all time, space, and dimensions. You will know when your space is clear and when love light flows.

After you bless your home and space, give thanks to the Creator, to all nature's intelligence, to the light, to the crystals, the feathers, the water, to the Earth Being, to all beings of light, to the archangels, angels, to all ascended masters, and to your divine guides. Thank you, Father Mother God.

All of life is serving us in holy ways. Honor all of life!

Always give thanks from your heart for all divine assistance—you are never walking alone. God's divine presence within you and in all life, your guardian angels, archangels, and divine guides are assisting you with infinite love and within God's light, heart, and consciousness. Invite and allow God's divine design of love to lead your path. You are living and breathing within a divine design and love light consciousness.

These words and prayers are guidelines for experiencing serenity and bliss in your space. Feel free to add any other words that are emphasizing and supporting your journey to embrace love and harmony.

When you pray, believe in your prayers. Allow all divine forces of love to lead your consciousness and way of life from your heart. The intentions you hold in your prayers are energies and consciousness in action.

> *The nature of my intentions embodies a leading creative force.*
> *I choose it to be godly, let go, and let God.*

Repeat the prayers several times. You will know when harmony is restored in your space and home—you will receive the experience of love.

Praying audibly often emphasizes the creative power of your prayers. Use these prayers any time you feel unease or when you wish to bring forth more of God's consciousness, love light within you and in your space.

PRAYING

Praying is about inviting and allowing the quintessence of life to reveal itself and to breathe in that holy space and consciousness. Praying is breathing love and speaking from my heart.

> *In my prayers, divine truth is revealed in me and expressed through me. It is offered to the world. The holiness of the world is then revealed back to me.*

Praying is learning about surrendering to all life. Praying is learning about God's qualities intrinsic to your true nature. It is learning about the holiness of your being. Praying is diving into the heart and mind of God. Praying is discovering your oneness and living in that truth.

Praying is loving life! Praying is praising life!

Praying is choosing to love and to be of service, touching one another lives in nurturing, honoring, and beautiful ways. It is recognizing holy consciousness emanating from within you, from within all beings, and all life. It is bathing in that flow and source of love, serenity, bliss, and plenitude.

It is allowing a nurturing space for the mind and the personality to work in synergy with the heart. It is opening the heart, allowing love's flow.

Praying is acknowledging sacred space and sacredness, empowering the realization of your true identity in love. When you are vibrating at higher frequencies, you have moved into higher consciousness. You will find yourself in a space where bliss and divine creativity unfold in infinity.

Praying is inviting and allowing the cosmic holy love light life force and divine creative potentialities to be revealed in your consciousness. Praying is allowing cosmic love light life force to lead the way.

With time and with practice, praying becomes a meditation, an experience of the love of God—a place of peace and grace. It becomes a way of life—a life of service, forever blissful, serene, and joyous. In prayer you are surrendering.

> *Praying is uniting my personality with the consciousness of my God-Self in harmony—breathing and living within a frequency of pure love—within the heart and mind of God.*
>
> *When my mental and emotional bodies are vibrating in harmonic synergy with the consciousness of the heart, my beingness is serene. I naturally experience the holy presence and the strength of Source within and without.*

The consciousness of the heart is the core consciousness of your being, of your divine presence. Your heart is the Stargate of the supreme love light sourcing from all creation—the love of God. Your heart is the stargate to the heart of creation, the heart of God.

> *Praying is expressing the consciousness of the heart.*
> *Praying is expressing my heart's desires and dreams.*
> *In my prayers I learn to love all beings and all life. I learn to love me.*
> *Prayers are guiding me through doorways of light, basking in the holiness and light of my being, discovering who I am in my deepest meditations.*
>
> *In my prayers, my heart speaks to God. In my prayers I learn*

to forgive and love myself—I learn to heal myself. I learn to
express myself with love. I learn to honor all creation.

THE MULTIPLE ASPECTS OF SURRENDERING— OF LETTING GO AND TRUSTING

Despite any difficulties, traumatic events, turmoil, or challenges in your life, you have the ability to surrender and to create positive changes. You have the ability to bring forth harmony and well-being by changing the way you perceive life.

At first, it is important to stop the fight. Stop fighting life! It is exhausting to fight life. It is exhausting striving to control your world through feelings of despair, feelings of never having enough, or feelings of not having what you wish for. It leads to increasing stress, depression, and despair, and the fight does not stop. You don't need to experience such pain.

Fear of the unknown may activate an obsessive behavior that is inimical to the full enjoyment of life. Since we are one with all of life, the unknown is a part of all life and its divine design. Since it is a divine design and you are one with it, the moment you are liberated from feelings of fears, divine love consciousness embraces you and works in oneness with you. Love the unknown, knowing its boundless gifts, opportunities, and abundance; you will feel uplifted, optimistic, and blissfully guided on your path.

Love the unknown as much as the flowers, the rainbows, the sun, and the rain, the animals, all beings, and all of creation. The unknown lives with us, and it is for us to welcome it as a loving friend with all its miraculous components. We can choose to see the unknown as an extraordinary doorway of light where we create in every moment (in the now), joy, well-being, beauty, and goodness in infinity.

When you accept the unknown as a good companion, you are

then living in the now. You are playing in the light, feeling happy to experience your true nature.

The unknown belongs to the magic of life—embrace it with joy!

When you stop fighting and embrace the present moment in peace, you stop identifying with the illusory aspect of life and all its turmoil. You discover who you are and experience your true identity. Your inner foundation is anchored in awareness, an awareness of your true divine nature. You are allowing the forces of love light emanating from all of life to naturally guide you and love you.

> *In my prayers I let go of all that is not in harmonic synergy with my God-Self. In my prayers I learn to love myself—I learn to love all beings.*
>
> *I allow, let go, and surrender right now. I choose to fully rejoice in the present moment and understand my gift and free will to choose love and appreciation now. I place myself in God's loving care.*
> *I direct my consciousness in my heart and invite God's consciousness to be expressed through me.*
> *Now and always, I choose to trust life and surrender to where my path is leading me with grace. I know that I am not walking alone. A supreme intelligence of unconditional love is guiding me to know my God-Self. I am safe, and I am loved. God's divine love is guiding my path now, and I allow it to be. I know who I am.*
>
> *Love is my path.*

Letting go is a feeling of great relief. It feels wonderful to let go. It welcomes bliss and serenity with the experience of your true nature. Letting go provides the space for you to create a new blissful reality.

Surrendering is making peace with life, living the eternal presence of your divinity. It is living and embracing inner divine guidance, allowing the forces of love light consciousness to guide your way, giving and receiving love with love, in love.

Surrendering and making peace with life does not mean that you agree with what is going on in your life and around you. It is not an opinion. It is an energy of unconditional love bliss and serenity, forever embracing with grace your life right now, exactly the way it is—free from all judgment.

Learn to see the presence of God beyond everything and then delve into the wisdom and understanding that is revealed to you. Delve into the essence and sacredness of life and learn to live from that frequency.

Contemplate your present life situation with your present state of mind as if you were watching a movie. It will help you to be less emotional, more realistic, and clearer about the awareness you wish to live in. You have the ability to understand your thoughts and experiences with awareness. You have the ability to allow and experience in your being any energetic frequency you wish since you are not your thoughts and experiences.

Which behavior do you wish to change? Which qualities do you wish to bring forth and express? Write a list about the changes, resolutions, and new directions you wish to create. Focus on the frequencies and the qualities of love you wish to project in order to create well-being and happiness in your life, within you and around you. Ask yourself the question: *How can I bring forth more goodness, peace, and love in me, in my life, and into the world?*

The highest qualities of love are already within you; they are a part of your fundamental essence.

All feelings of despair create an energetic veil so dense that it blocks your inner vision from seeing truth and seeing who you are. Criticizing in a judgmental way lowers your frequencies. Be aware of your perception because it does not always reflect truth. Live from the heart consciousness—be an observer or witness. Practice equanimity.

Divine guidance is always available to you, but it is difficult to embrace it and be aware of it if you are in a state of continuing turmoil and despair. Calm down and breathe deeply and slowly in your heart. Move your consciousness within and learn to be conscious of your breathing. In meditation, dive into the consciousness of your true divine being.

The more you struggle, the more you force, push, and fight life, the more you block the intrinsic energy flow of goodness, harmony, and well-being. You block the energetic, creative flow of love. Your ego and your thoughts are running your life. In such circumstances, you feel increasingly more hopeless, helpless, confused, and trapped. You feel mentally, emotionally, and physically weak and exhausted. You are unable to take action—or if you take action, you are not vibrating at a high frequency. You feel helpless because you have been away from the experience of who you are. You have been away from home. You have been away from the beautiful and magnificent being you are. You have forgotten your God-Self and life's sacredness. Now is the time to remember!

Practice daily, nurturing feelings of gratefulness. Gratefulness represents a powerful energy of fullness, abundance, wellness, and goodness. Direct your attention to your blessings and express gratitude. You will naturally attract more of what you are grateful for. Practice being present and connect with your inner holy consciousness.

Slowly build up a quiet and peaceful place within. Allow all thoughts to dissipate so that you have the ability to welcome the true consciousness of your divine beingness. Awaken to the beauty of your world, honor all life, and make peace with all of life. You are surrendering.

As I surrender, the innate ability to experience peace love light in my vibrational frequency is awakened. I discover the qualities of my soul and I experience God.

It is from a place of complete letting go and humility that

I open a space allowing the creation of a new reality for myself, embracing with consciousness the true nature of my beingness.

When you are hopeful it is easier to surrender and trust. When hope is leading to feelings of trust, you are already surrendering and opening up to inner peace and grace. If hope is leading back to struggling, it is because you are caught into the "despair and being separated" syndrome—ego and thoughts are then still controlling your life.

I now choose to live the experience of peace love light consciousness emanating from the core of my being, in synergy with the peace love light emanating from all of creation, forever holding me in sacredness. I am safe! I am loved! I am love! I am light! I surrender with ease and grace to the Divine Living Presence—I experience peace and bliss.

All of these steps are leading to surrendering. When you surrender you are also moving toward a state of equanimity. Equanimity is an experience that is liberating, free from all criticism and judgment, revealing your divinity and multidimensionality.
Learn to liberate your mind from all human thought forms to invite divine knowledge and consciousness.

Surrendering is being free from all feelings of struggle, despair, and judgment. It is experiencing well-being, bliss, and serenity.

Surrendering is an amazing feeling of freedom that is empowering, comforting, and nurturing, leading to an awakening of your heart's qualities of love. Surrendering leads to an awakening of your purpose and mission—your true path is unfolding.

When you surrender, you naturally move your consciousness in the heart. You bring forth energies of love, joy, and harmony in all that you do. These beautiful energies are received by all beings and by all of creation. You are allowing creative harmonic synergies to flow into your existence.

When you feel serene, you are surrendering.

Surrendering leads to compassion. Compassion is a state of awareness, understanding, and complete forgiveness. In compassion, the heart opens to express unconditional love. Compassion holds a space of reverence that is nurturing, loving, and free from all judgment.

The process of surrendering is learning to trust life and see truth. You are then with your authentic Self. When you are in touch with your authentic Self—and honoring your authentic Self—you are on your way to serve all life in divine ways.

Surrendering is opening an inner gateway, inviting an awareness of God. In the process of surrendering you become devoted to love. You are diving into blissful serenity.

SURRENDERING, ALLOWING, CREATING, AND MANIFESTING FROM LOVE, THROUGH LOVE, AND IN LOVE • LIVING FROM A CONSCIOUSNESS OF THE HEART

As I surrender I discover the consciousness of my heart. Learning to live from a consciousness of the heart in all that you do, feel, think and speak is allowing the highest energies of serenity, harmony, honoring, praise, love, and joy to guide your path. It is transmuting low frequencies into high love light frequencies. You are emanating a radiant light that is reaching all of life. Light invites light. Love invites love. Love is light and light is love.

Your "unified" heart is activated when you choose to love all beings and all life—when you choose to be in service for the highest good of all creation—when the personality and mind welcomes all qualities of the one sacred heart.

The light body awakens from the unified heart by working in oneness and in synergetic light patterns within infinite cosmic divine love encompassing the heart and mind of God. A holy ray of light illuminates the brain (mind), the pineal gland, pituitary glands, and chakras (energy centers), encompassing all aspects of your being reaching the cells, DNA/RNA, all bodies, and fields. True consciousness and divine knowledge are revealed and expressed.

Your heart is the central sun of your "beingness" where peace love light consciousness, true consciousness, and holy consciousness originate.

From your illuminated heart and from your illuminated mind you have the ability to experience the heart and mind of God. This process is activated when your intentions are pure, when you choose to love all life, and when you surrender.

You are then allowing, creating, and manifesting from love, through love, and in love.

When you surrender, you contribute to peace and activate love energies wherever you go. Your heart is open, and you are inspiring others to open their hearts and trust. The power of divine love sourcing from the heart is boundless.

Learn to live with consciousness and love life in every moment! Celebrate in joy!

Joy flows endlessly in my being and my life!

Decide to make everything playful in your life. It brings good feelings and good energies in all that you do. Everything becomes fun—even cleaning your home. If you clean your home with joy, this joyous vibration is going to be present within all your belongings, and walls, and floors, and roof, creating an uplifting energy that harmonizes and brings forth a sense of comfort and well-being. It is similar to a clearing process. Play all day long. It is uplifting. It is joy! Try and you will see! Joy is another aspect of surrendering. When you feel joy you naturally let go of energies that are not yours—you raise your frequencies and embrace your true being.

Life loves me. God loves me. I remember who I am. I am joy!

Do not be hard on yourself if you think that you made a mistake because in reality there are no mistakes. Instead of judging and criticizing, look for the wisdom and the bliss in the experience. Learn from it and move on. We often dramatize situations. Often, the mind takes over and we move away from true consciousness. Look for the blessings in your experiences and challenges.

Drama is a toxic addiction that feeds the ego. It is important to step out of it. Surrender! In reality, there is nothing to be upset about. Life is really very simple when we choose to forgive, live from the heart and express love, compassion, gratitude, and reverence. It is a conscious commitment and choice to live within the consciousness of our holy presence and the holiness in all life. It is awareness. It is a nurturing energy of love that is unconditional.

I have come to believe that the "secret" is the art to always respond to life with love in love. It is of grace.

*Love flows in all aspects of my life! I experience the energies
of love in my heart, in all my being, relationships and affairs.
I smile at life! Life loves me.*

In your willingness to thrive, bring forth all qualities of the heart and create a beautiful life from a consciousness of love.

Acknowledge, invite, and embrace the embodiment of the universal true power of love sourcing from all of creation—Father Mother God—to be the force that is nurturing you, loving you, and guiding your way.

Activating the heart consciousness invites the light body to exude its light.

Surrendering in Prayer and Meditation

You don't need to leave your friends and family, living secluded for years to find illumination, fulfillment, serenity, bliss, and happiness, although that is a choice. The school of enlightenment is right where you are now.

Learn to be still and serene within. In daily meditations, listen to the voice within you and within all forms. The sacredness of life reveals itself naturally.

Meditating is reaching deep inside to discover and experience your true divine nature. It is learning to hear and see from a holy place, from your God-Self—from the heart and mind of God.
Meditation leads to blissful serenity and clarity. With time, meditation takes you to an ecstatic experience of oneness.
In meditation, discover the creative power to manifest through love. Meditation clears all the clutter within the mind and from your field. It opens a doorway, a new space of bliss, serenity, love, and light. It reveals a space to create and to be inspired in divine ways.

Meditating is listening to the voice of God within—within the silence and stillness of your being. It is an energetic emanation that is bountiful in love, transcending all time, space, and levels of life.

Practicing meditation is gently moving your consciousness toward a new paradigm of freedom and harmony. Meditation is a state of complete letting go, free from pain and struggle. It is being the leaf dancing with the wind, effortlessly moving with the flow of life. It is allowing divine loving guidance to gently show you the way. It is a complete state of freedom, ease, and grace.

Meditation is living in the sacredness of "your presence". You discover who you are. In the sacredness of your presence, you know that you are held in holiness.

With time, your meditations are becoming deeper and deeper. The experiences of bliss, serenity, and joy are increasing. You are discovering your God-Self, your true Self, and your oneness with all of life. It is love!

Meditate on the beauty and divine synergies sourcing from all of life. Experience the flow of love within and without as one consciousness.

One evening, as I was meditating on feelings of surrendering, I was asking in my heart, for a special message that would support the process of surrendering and feeling safe within and with all of life—connecting with the essence of life. The next morning, as I was slowly emerging from my slumber, as I was gently embraced by light, this message was given to me: *All life is loving, and I bathe myself in that source of love, now and always.*

During that night, the angels invited me to sing with them: *Om, I am Elohim!*

The melodies, voices, and sounds were of divine beauty! I always have wanted to sing like that—and now I knew I could! The angels said: *All that is of love shall be yours!* It was an experience of Heaven, basking in God's love light and the holy sounds of the hymns. It was boundless love consciousness.

My heart was filled with so much warmth, love, and gratitude. I kept repeating these words. As I was walking in nature with my beautiful dog, I was living the words. A flow of love kept rising from my heart with a profound sense of oneness. I felt safe and nurtured experiencing the love sourcing from all of life.

These very simple words became one of my most beloved mantras. I especially enjoy falling asleep experiencing the energy of the words. These simple words are helping transmute fear into love. They calm the ego and lead the personality to love and peace.

HOW IS "SURRENDERING" RESPONDING TO YOUR PHYSICAL BODY?

Your physical body has its own consciousness and its own intelligence. Honor your physical body and create a loving and nurturing relationship with your physical body so that with your soul you may walk through life with grace and feeling good.

As you surrender, you have the ability to lovingly harmonize your physical body along with the emotional and mental bodies. Learn to be aware of your breathing. Focusing on your breathing is initially a support to free the mind, let go, relax, and meditate. Awareness of your breathing and practicing breathing exercises increase your life force energy. They are calming and balancing the energy flow, moving through your body and field. They also help you to be present, whole, and grounded.

Start your meditation by breathing deeply and slowly until you calm the mind. Breathe throughout your whole body and command your mind and body to calm down and relax. As your mind calms, your body relaxes. Become the breath and calm the breath. Nothing exists other that the breath of God living in you. The breath is a soft breeze of peace love light, moving through you and nurturing you. Give yourself time to experience this.

In another meditation, breathe with consciousness the love of God in your heart. Expand the love light sourcing from the heart, all around you. Feel this love and light sourcing from within you and from all life. As you breathe in this holy energy, relax and massage your brain, your eyes, your face, your neck, your arms, your muscles, your organs, and your whole body with that loving light energy emanating from your breath. Breathe peace love light in all aspect of your being, including your blood, energy centers, cells, DNA/RNA, bodies, and fields. Breathe peace love light from the top of your head all the way under your feet (experience your bond with the Earth Being). Move your breathing back to the top of your head, and into the palms of your hands. Then, breathe love in your heart and hold that serene place for a few moments.

Practice various breathing exercises. They activate the love light life force that is reawakening from the core of your being. You have the ability to increase your "chi" or "life force energy" and heal yourself if you are looking for any level of healing.

If you wish to have more support, you may attend a class that focuses on the breath. It can also be a yoga class where you will practice the breath of fire and diverse breathing techniques. You have the ability to learn diverse breathing patterns, which strengthen your mind and body. They enhance your health and calm your emotions, offering you peace and clarity. Such breathing techniques also enhance and support the qualities of your meditations. They bring forth a wonderful support to the process of surrendering.

Surrendering is making peace with all aspects of your beingness and all of creation. It is letting go of the fight, of the despair, of the judgment, of the self-pity, of the resentment. It is a calming energy that balances the cells in your physical body. It is letting go of all that does not belong to you.

Surrendering increases your life force and harmonizes the energies of your cells, all your bodies, and fields. You will notice tensions, aches, and pains in your physical body fading away and disappearing.

As you let go, it becomes easier to attend lovingly to your physical form, since you have become more attuned with the energetic emanation of your being. As your mind experiences serenity and stillness, you are naturally tuned into your physical, emotional, and spiritual vibrational frequency. It becomes easier to locate energetic disharmony within your body and activate energetic harmonization and realignment. As you are surrendering, you are experiencing the love light life force energizing your whole being—from the core of your being and cells.

As you surrender, the love light life force is activated from within, adjusting, repairing, harmonizing, and energizing any frequency within the cells, organs, energy centers, fields, and bodies that have been depleted of love life force.

The physical body has often been compared to a temple or an altar of the soul. I like to think of it as such, honoring its sacredness. Honoring the sacredness of the physical body is to honor its divine purpose. It is taking care of it in nurturing loving ways.

> *The radiating light and life of my divine spirit dances in harmonic synergy with my body temple's divine design and purpose. I breathe life with joy.*

Your physical body feels good and your mind is blissful when you are honoring all of "you".

Your physical body has a consciousness serving the highest purpose, contributing to the progress of the soul. As you make peace within and with all life, the light of your whole being awakes.

> *I digest life and food with ease, love, and peace.*

Close your eyes and connect with your physical body. Observe how it feels. Breathe with consciousness while scanning your whole body. Pay attention to how your body feels. Breathe in your physical body and connect with its frequency. Scan your whole body, always conscious of the breathing. Does your body feel tense? Are your muscles relaxed or tight? Do you feel good or unease? Is your breath deep and serene or short? Do you feel stressed out? Which part of your body is hurting? Do you feel serene, blissful, and relaxed?
If you pay attention, you will realize that your body speaks to you.

Your emotional and mental bodies are energetically interconnected and energetically unified with the physical body. Your emotions, thoughts, words, intentions, and beliefs are energetically reflected in your physical structure.

The more you spend time in touch with the consciousness of your true identity or presence, the more serene, healthy, and happy you will be.

The energetic frequency of the body and capacity of life force is initiated by the nature of the frequencies you choose to emanate from thoughts, intentions, and feelings—as well as from programs embedded in the cells, DNA, and RNA.

Are you pushing yourself? Are you resentful? Are you frustrated? Are you harsh on yourself? Are you fighting life? Are you jealous? Are you judging others? If you experience any of these feelings and patterns, your body is most likely tense and probably hurting. These feelings are expressing a sense of lack that is not real. These fear-based energies reflect your perception of yourself and the world around you. None of them reflect the reality of your true Self and of your oneness with life. Surrender!

Are you able to move with the flow of life with ease? Are you compassionate? Are you in love with life? Do you walk in life from a place of ongoing struggle? Do you judge yourself and others?
See if you are able to locate negative feelings, beliefs, resentment, worry, stress, frustration, anger, or any other emotional pattern that is causing a specific part of your body to hurt. Look for this sense of lacking and fear you have been holding within you so that you can recognize it, release it, and transmute the energy into a frequency of compassion and love. Learn to get in touch with your feelings so that you are able to let go of the ones that are not serving you. Fill that space with unconditional love. Make conscious choices.

> *I release into the light of God all that is not serving my highest good. My whole being is suffused with the love and light of God.*

Locate all areas of your physical body that are feeling good. Rest, breathing consciously in that energy. Feel this nurturing energy through your whole body.

Meditate and focus on your breath. Move into an awareness of your presence. Ask to be guided to see and experience the "true you", the nature of your essence.

Seek help from a spiritual practitioner if you are not able to release pain. Sometimes pain is so deeply embedded in the memory of the cells that we need help to understand it, release it, transform it, and bring in positive energies and positive reprogramming. It is possible to release and heal psychosomatic issues. It is an energetic shift of consciousness. Your state of mind and how you respond to life are intimately related to how you feel physically.

Talk to your cells and to your whole being in nurturing and loving ways. For example, in meditation, ask your cells to be filled with vibrant love light life force energy and joy. Ask that they be harmoniously connected with one another. Ask them, to have a happy journey together! *I am allowing this now.*

Your physical vibrational frequency is in synergy with the nature of the consciousness you choose. If you believe that you will develop pain and illness, your body will gradually respond to these beliefs and low vibrations. If you believe that you are going to get weak and ill as you become older, you are vibrationally building up that reality. If you dwell on negativity, your breath becomes shallow and you may feel anxious, weak, depleted, tired, and sick. With time, your physical body becomes depleted of life force. Your magnetic energetic field becomes scattered. You are inviting additional low and unbalanced energies into your space. You are separating yourself from all of who you are.
Choose to go back to the heart of your divine presence! Choose to go back to your Self.

Physical challenges may appear difficult to overcome, although they can be true gifts. Physical challenges are opportunities to get in touch with your true Self and heal from the inside out, so that you may step into the experience of your energetic divine essence and the essence of life. In meditation, enter and explore the foundation, the core of your being, to reach the ultimate experience of freedom and light within. In that freedom, the physical body moves into balance and harmony as well as all bodies and fields—allowing love light life force to be activated from within.

And if ever it is time for you to move onto another blissful journey and leave your physical body, you will leave free, bathing in divine love and light.

Exercise, run, walk, swim, dance, practice yoga, move the body, breathe consciously throughout your whole body, spend time in nature, eat healthy, meditate and love life! Be of help to others with love! Your physical health will improve greatly, you will feel whole, and you will be happy.

Spending time in nature is the best and easiest place to meditate, exercise, and rejuvenate. However, in reality, it is possible to meditate, rejuvenate, and experience wellness and wholeness anywhere. The key is in your ability to focus and develop your willingness through love from the core center of your being, in the heart of your soul. **In the awareness of the holiness of your presence, love consciousness flows and expands from the heart of the soul—and from the heart of all hearts.**

Choose to play—invite laughter, humor, and joy in your life. They are a source of wellness. Step into the heart consciousness of life and dance within that consciousness.

At those times when you are seeking emotional support, expand your consciousness to a new reality—where there is no memory other than your true energetic nature of unconditional love. Focus on your breathing and meditate. *I breathe in the heart of God. I bathe in the light of God.*

Feel the light and love of God permeating your whole being.

Learn to experience the life force and divinity of your being. Surrender. Ask for balance, love, and harmony. Bask in the love and light of God. Trust divine intervention. Ask Source to teach you how to receive boundless nurturing love and wellness. Learn to receive with ease, grace, joy, and gratitude. Breathe in your whole being and energy field the divine light and love of God (all the way to your cells) all the way to your feet and under your feet—experience your bond of love with the Earth Being and with all life. Express infinite gratitude and praise.

As a spiritual practitioner, I have witnessed many people healed physically and emotionally as they were completely letting go of their struggles and challenges, placing themselves in God's loving care. It has happened to me on several occasions. These prayers, insights, and meditations support such experience. Practice! Discover and explore your multidimensionality and spirituality!

You do not need to believe what others believe. You do not need to create what other people choose to create. People respond to life by activating specific vibrational perceptions and patterns, creating their reality in every moment.

There is a magnetic flow of energy that each one of us chooses, allows and emanates. The nature and frequency of that energy influences all levels of our lives, as well as the flow of life force within the physical body.
You have the freedom to choose your beliefs and the way you respond to life. You are a creative being.

All sense of lack and despair is coming from fear, the mind, and ultimately the ego. It is an energy that is not real and does not belong to you in any way. See this energy separated from you and ask that it be released into the Light of God. Move your consciousness in your heart, pray and meditate. Bask into the nectar of life, a realm of unconditional love encompassing all that is.

> *I bask in God's boundless source of love. I am protected and loved now and forever.*
> *It is safe for me to shine my light! I feel safe and wonderful to allow God's divine love consciousness to lead my path*

because I know my source. I listen to the voice of love and act accordingly.

What is holding you back from feeling love, loved, and happy? Are your thoughts and beliefs keeping you victimized and confined?

You might think: *If I feel happy, I show a lack of compassion for all the beings who are suffering. I cannot allow myself to feel good when others are suffering.*
It does not work this way! If you deprive yourself of feeling good and happy, you are not helping anybody—and you are depriving the world of your love, your joy, your gifts, and your light. You are depriving yourself of knowing your true Self, of thriving, of serving life's highest purposes, of contributing to a world of peace, of expanding and growing and learning! You are depriving yourself of knowing all the love, light, beauty, and joy you are born to express, receive, and give. Your physical body is then deprived of life force too.
You are a sacred being—it is safe and divine to shine your light. Your light is a gift of love to the world. Learn to exude peace, qualities of love, compassion, and joy to participate in a better world. Your physical body will be very happy to welcome this energy.

The world does not need more sorrow. The world is eager to embrace your love and gifts, support you, and lead you in nurturing ways on your journey.
Live in harmonic synergy with the nature of your true identity.

Your physical body with your whole beingness naturally embraces your positive, loving, and nurturing energies within its cosmic energetic divine design.

Some people say: *I will never give up the fight. I will fight this disease.*
As long as you choose to fight, you are projecting energies of struggle and sometimes of despair. You are projecting an energy that separates you from your God-Self. Projecting energies of struggle or despair blocks the flow of love light and negates your ability toward wellness.

By holding on to such low energy, you are interrupting the natural flow of life force moving through your being and emerging from the core of your being. You are interrupting the life force natural synergy. You are one with all life force.

If you sustain such low and disruptive vibrations of struggle and despair, love light life force is not able to be expressed fully and move harmoniously through your cells, bodies, and fields as it is naturally destined to do so—restoring or sustaining a natural balance.

Surrendering in love and freeing the mind is living within the natural consciousness and essence of your being. You are then allowing the natural flow of love light life force to express itself through all aspects of your being. All energies that are not a match to the true nature of your essence are then naturally liberated into the light, or immediately harmonized by the light. You feel light and clear. Your light shines. You know who you are—there is nothing to fear anymore.

Divine love light is now moving through my cells, bodies, and fields— reprogramming, repairing, and activating all life force—restoring, awakening all harmonic flow.
I feel and see God's love and light moving through me and around me, nurturing me. I smile and embrace love light with joy!

I now chose to live within the consciousness of the essence of my being.
I know my source. I know who I am.
I am activating my body of light! I am activating a new world of peace!

It is never too late to surrender and choose wellness and happiness. Time and space are boundless and sempiternal.

Seek God Within •
Open your Heart to God's Love

In every moment, you are creating. Surrendering is also learning to create in love. It is allowing receiving from God or Source. It is a gift because when you receive from God, you also give from a holy place of God's consciousness. You are then expressing unconditional love. Choose to give, receive, and serve all life in love.

How do you receive from God? When you decide to be true to you! When you surrender and love all of life! When you allow the embodiment of love consciousness to nurture you, to hold you, and to lead your way—when you choose to be of service. When you love "all of you". When you allow your true Self to be revealed and shine. When you allow the consciousness of the heart to be revealed and expressed. When you live in faith, inviting God's infinite qualities to be expressed through you. When you discover boundless blissful serenity and joy within the stillness of your being—and when you learn to live from that consciousness.
Receiving from the Creator is the ultimate gift of love.

Knowing how to give with love is receiving love. Knowing how to receive with love is giving love.

> *I awaken my consciousness to all of creation, the sempiternity presence of a cosmic divine intelligence holding a holy consciousness of love.*
> *I invite all the qualities of the Creator to be boundlessly expressed from within me and through me. I surrender in love.*
> *I am a multidimensional divine being, a source of infinite divine knowledge, love, and light.*

Open your heart to God's consciousness, and you shall receive from a bountiful power of love.

I live in the supreme heart and mind of God. This is my true expression. This is who I am. Every day I further surrender to discover who I am and to experience the heart and mind of God.

I would like to share with you a beautiful experience that occurred to me related to trust and receiving from God. I was coming from a place of surrender and faith. Many years ago, I visited my parents in Zermatt, Switzerland, for a couple of weeks. I was looking forward to visiting them in this beautiful place. Ever since the time of my childhood and as I was growing up I spent every summer vacation in Zermatt with my parents and sisters. It was a very relaxing and magical time for all of us.

That particular year, however, I was coming out from a painful experience that had left me emotionally broken. I knew I had to learn many lessons from that experience, and I would grow stronger. I would grow stronger in my awareness, wisdom, and faith. I knew that I was in the process of moving closer to an inner divine truth and to God. We always are! I was committed to sustaining gentle feelings of compassion toward myself to allow the releasing and harmonizing process. It was a healing process of surrendering, of complete letting go. I was committed to the releasing process, allowing whatever time it would take to be free and back home to my true Self.

My joyous energy was gone, and everything was hurting inside me, including my physical body. Even though I was infinitely grateful to be able to visit with my parents and felt blessed to be back in one of my favorite place on Earth, I could not get my joy, balance, and energy back. I felt depleted and powerless over these feelings. I knew that my condition would not last, and I had to surrender and place my whole Self in the loving care of God, and trust—this is what I did.

When I arrived in Zermatt, I noticed that my dad was losing his vital energy, experiencing sadness and depression. He was losing weight and was barely eating. Since the passing of his youngest brother, several months ago, he had progressively fallen into a deeper depression. When I saw him in this condition, my first desire was to help him through healing energy work. I was so depleted that I had no mental strength to do so, since I was not fully connected within—and this situation created even more sadness in me. I felt emotionally lost, too broken and too weak to do anything. The only hope and comfort I could find were in my prayers and meditations.

I prayed for hours and hours, especially at night when I was alone in my room. Zermatt is a sacred and holy place to me; just to be within that energy was somehow comforting.

Every night, my mother and I were observing white glowing lights above the little city and above the mountains surrounding the city. I could feel that these glowing lights were divine and angelic presences to assist humankind and the Earth Being. I knew that they are usually seeing in holy and sacred places around the world (you may read additional insights about the spheres of light in chapter 5—Secret and Sacredness of Life).

One morning, I woke up around four o'clock. From my bed and through my window, I could see the mountains covered with snow. That night, just above the mountain, I observed two large spheres of light. To ease my pain I was praying, always contemplating the bright lights. As I was praying, I felt love in my heart. I prayed to God to bless my parents and to restore my strength and balance, to make me whole again so that I could be a vessel of light to assist my father in his healing through God's loving, divine guidance. I just knew in my heart that the help would come directly from God, from the love sourcing from all life, and from within me. I knew that no one could help me with this—other than my direct connection with God, with the Creator, the Divine within me within all life.

I prayed and prayed while observing the vortices of light. Suddenly, a double rainbow emerged from the two lights, forming a spiral moving toward me reaching my heart center. A state of bliss came all over me. I kept praying. I finally fell asleep and woke up a few hours later. It was daylight, and the spheres of light were gone. Even as I was still feeling the pain, I just knew that something significant would happen. I had great faith in experiencing my wholeness again, and especially being able to help my father.

I was praying all the time, even in silence during the day. The following night, I was visualizing myself within a double tetrahedron (two tetrahedrons join at their base) of crystal light to find some loving comfort and release. In my prayers, I was placing myself in God's loving care. This was an energetic visualization—I was practicing every night to find peace and love. In my meditation, I felt divine, loving presences and was fully awake. Suddenly my soul moved out of my physical body. I could have stopped the movement, but I was feeling so safe and so loved that I let it happen. It was too painful to be in my physical body at that time. I was welcoming any spiritual experience that could be a release of my sorrow. I moved through the wall and in the air, far away into the sky. I felt loved, safe, and protected.

I arrived in another place in time and within higher dimensional realms. This is what it felt like. I landed on a boardwalk by the immensity of a sea. The water was a deep turquoise. In the distance, on a deck, there were a few people standing. I was wondering if they would see me because I was aware of traveling without my physical body, in spirit form. We moved toward one another. One man started talking to me telepathically. I knew that they were in spirit form, too. He said to me in French: "Welcome! We are so happy for your visit and we hope to see you again." I smiled at him and thanked him. Afterward, I was gently uplifted in the air. I felt completely guided, loved, and safe. I felt I was in a familiar environment. As I was moving in the air I saw a few small flying objects with wings, similar to bird wings. These wings were attached on both sides of what appeared to be a mechanical object. I also saw a few airborne people moving in different directions.

I was guided to a place I knew was holy. The place felt very familiar. It was like a sacred sanctuary. I was standing, my arms along my body and my palms facing forward. Suddenly, at the level of my heart center, I was filled with an infinite flow of love and light force energy. My heart was filled with the most perfect, unconditional blissful love and light force energy moving through my whole beingness. It was like a glowing stream of love light endlessly moving in me and through me. As I was being filled with this divine love light force energy, I said over and over again, "Thank you. Thank you. Thank you." The experience of release, healing, blissful serenity, and pure love was extraordinary and ecstatic.

I had no idea how long it lasted. When it stopped, I was guided to another location within the same sacred sanctuary, and the same experience happened again. I was filled with the most delicious, ecstatic, perfect love light energy. I had no idea how long it lasted. I was completely filled and embraced by that incredible love light holy force energy. I would have liked to stay in that moment forever; it was so delightful and sublime. Feeling the love in my heart, I was repeating in the blissful serenity of my being, "Thank you. Thank you!"

I was guided to move out of the sanctuary when a gentle voice said it was time to go back. I visited for a little longer, moving in the air. I traveled through time and space to come back gently into my physical body. When I came back, I placed my hands over my heart and in the serenity of my being expressed gratefulness, "Thank you Father Mother God. Thank you to all light beings. Thank you to all life. Thank you. Thank you!"

I knew that I could help my father. I was whole again. My life force was back. I was experiencing blissful serenity. My whole being was balanced, bathing in love light and serene.

The next day, at the most appropriate time when my father was ready to go to sleep, I asked him if he would allow me to proceed with a healing on him. He was all right with it. I created a sacred space by asking and inviting God's divine assistance, the love and light of God, my divine guidance team, masters of light and of the white brotherhood, the angels of light, the archangels, and my father's divine guidance team. I placed my hands a few inches over my father's body to proceed with the clearing and harmonizing of his energy field for the healing to take place.

We were divinely guided throughout the whole healing process. There were many hands of light involved in the process. Among these hands of light, I was guided to move my hands in the air in specific ways, allowing God's love light to come forth, clearing and harmonizing my father's energy field and bodies. I held the intention to send into the light of God all energies that did not belong to him, including earthbound spirits or any other energetic life form, pain and traumas that may be blocking light, with great love, peace, compassion, and gentleness.

Through the grace, love, and light of God, with the divine guidance team, all openings in my father's auric field were now sealed with light love energy. This is from where he was losing his vital energy and from where he was inviting in energies that were not his. I asked for all unbalanced energies, in all time, space, and dimensions, on all levels, reaching all his bodies and field, cells and DNA/RNA to be transmuted into love light life force and harmonized by God's light. I asked that he be showered by God's supreme love light force, blessings, and infinite grace. I asked for loving harmonization of his energy centers, bodies, and field, reaching his cells, and DNA/RNA. It was energy light work.

When I witnessed the light of God moving through his whole being and saw the glow of his auric field, I knew that he was whole and well. Throughout the healing session he had fallen into a deep sleep. I was in such gratitude to be of service again. I gave thanks to God and to all the beings of light for all the love and divine assistance. I went into my room with a deep sense of serenity and gratefulness in my heart.

In the following days, I saw my father transform. His appetite came back to normal. He was feeling good and more cheerful. I understood the great gifts and blessings we received throughout the whole experience.
I also prayed for my mother to be blessed with serenity and God's love. I knew that she had been worried about my father.

From spirit, I received permission from my father to share this story with you. I hope that this experience inspires you. When you surrender to God's love consciousness inherently embedded within all of life—when you know your heart consciousness of love light, goodness, and harmony—when you wish to be of service to all life—when faith is truly anchored in your heart, a sacred space of love opens in the most surprising holy ways. Doorways of light open!

We are never walking alone. There are no limits of what you may experience when you open your heart to receive from God.

Faith opens doorways of love light! I had faith despite all the pain. I knew that this pain was an energy that will fade away, and that it was a transitory state guiding me to a new level of awareness and grace. I knew in my heart that my prayers would be answered. The faith in my heart was clear and strong. I was surrendering in an awareness of God's love light consciousness leading the way. I didn't know how the situation would evolve, but I knew that it would source from the highest place of love. Faith opened a space for divine will to be revealed and for divine love to express itself.

When you surrender to God, you receive in holy ways. Learn to receive from your heart in holy ways.
Circumstances in life had created such pain in my beingness, guiding me to move closer to God—closer to my God-Self.

If you choose to run away from painful feelings by using drugs or any other harmful addictions, pain will stay with you. Pain will then take over your life since you are moving away from your true identity. The mind takes over. Negative thoughts and feelings, with the ego, are running the show of your life. Pain will come back into your face until you surrender and create a shift in consciousness by connecting with the true nature of your being.

Surrendering, allowing, creating, and manifesting in love is experienced in the awareness of your divinity. You are living a loving nurturing relationship with all of life, with all that is, with all beings, and with "you".

In this chapter, I have presented guidelines leading to surrendering. These guidelines are leading your prayers and wishes into new dimensions of light to be answered in the most unexpected, holy, and marvelous ways. You are opening a space of love that is unlimited, revealing wonders of life—creating and expanding in harmony and love.

My wish is that these guidelines inspire you to surrender and to navigate within the infinite consciousness of your inner being with grace.

When pain is brought into your life, it is always a gift for you to move closer to God. It is a part of you that expresses the wish to release energies that are not yours—and have been with you, sometimes for a long time. It is your whole beingness wishing for further harmony and energetic alignment through love. Do not judge yourself. See what is given to you with awareness and grace. Be the witness and allow the process! Proceed with the spiritual inner work you need to do. Look for the gift, for the wisdom.

When you place yourself in God's loving care and trust, everything is possible. You are inviting the vastness and multidimensionality of life to be expressed in divine ways.

Surrendering in your Personal Sacred Sanctuary

The following insights are guiding you to create your personal sacred sanctuary. In meditation and visualization, create a nurturing and serene oasis of love that is empowering to you and healing you. Imagine your sacred place as beautiful and magical as you wish—on a beach, in the mountains, in a meadow—there are no limits—**ask it to be or declare it to be the realm of God's consciousness—joy, blissful serenity, love, and beauty.** Invite God's bountiful love and light, archangels and angels of light, divine beings of light, fairies, unicorns, and your master guides of light, any animals you wish, anyone and anything you wish that represent nurturing love light to you.

Become aware of the divine living presence, the radiant light, and the pure love within your haven. Breathe deeply and slowly that holy energy—in your whole being. Feel the love in your heart. Feel this love connecting with the warm, loving energies all around you, emanating from all life. Invite in the colors of the rainbow or any ray of light you are being guided to embrace in your space. Color lights are healing and sustain specific energetic qualities. Get in touch with your heart's desires to create from a place of boundless grace, love, and joy.

Your sacred sanctuary is a place within you. It represents your secret garden—a paradise you step into and visit when you wish to resource yourself—when you wish to consciously connect with the sacredness of life to find strength, comfort, vitality, and joy—when you wish to bathe more consciously in God's light and love—when you wish to reconnect with your true Self and come back to awareness—when you wish to create and co-create from God consciousness, releasing and allowing—when you wish to have a good time playing in the light.

I am divine light, forever creating and expanding in love.

Your beautiful, sacred sanctuary is the perfect place to visualize and experience your dreams and prayers. Enjoy the energies.
In you sanctuary, between your prayers and visualization, calm the mind and let go of thoughts—take time to meditate and experience peace love and your light. Experience peace love light emanating from all life surrounding you.

Your beautiful magical sanctuary is a place where you feel safe, nurtured, loved, and supported by all life. It is a place that is so nurturing and so holy that you feel safe to let go and experience healing, well-being, wellness, and harmony. God's peace love light is permeating your whole being and consciousness. You are experiencing unconditional love and joy.

It is a place where you have the tools to step away from your thoughts to calm your emotions—and the ego is at rest. By doing so, you create a space to experience the sacredness of life and divine guidance. You are allowing the forces of peace love light to inspire you and gently guide your way—to step into a new paradigm that is serene and blissful where you meet the real you. It is a consciousness inviting you to be creative in divine ways—to understand your purpose and your mission.

Every time you leave your sacred sanctuary and move on with your day, you bring with you the same energies you have created in your paradise. The creative visualization and energies of peace, love, and joy you have been nurturing in your sanctuary are emanating from you wherever you are—reaching all of life. All creative visualizations have been energetically empowered in your sacred sanctuary.

In your beautiful sacred sanctuary, you are discovering and exploring divine unlimited qualities embedded in the consciousness of your true Self and in all life. Explore all realms of consciousness with reverence, honoring, infinite love, and sacredness.

In your sanctuary, it is easy to move into full awareness of the present moment. Take time to be fully conscious of the energies of light and love surrounding you. You are living a vision of a sacred place you are creating that is nurturing you.

In your sanctuary, feel love, reverence, and gratefulness for the Earth Being, all its beauty, bliss, and gifts, and for all its inhabitants from all realms. Witness light expanding from your heart in all four directions above and below, reaching all life around you in your sanctuary. With time, you will feel whole in your sanctuary—you will experience your light, divinity, and wholeness in your life. In your sanctuary you are learning to live aware of the sacredness of life, revering all life.

In your sacred sanctuary, experience nurturing loving energies of light expanding limitlessly. From your heart, your light is expanding throughout the whole planet and beyond. Feel the love emanating from all creation. When you are ready, come back into your sacred space gently, experiencing the love. Place your hands on your heart center and feel love emanating from your heart. Take as much time as you wish to enjoy your journey. Rejoice and play in your sanctuary. Play in the light.

Bathe consciously in God's love light before leaving your sanctuary. Always express gratefulness to Source, to all life, and all you have invited in your sacred sanctuary. Thank all the beautiful beings of light, angels, archangels, and nature's spirits such as fairies and devas (consciousness living within the plants, trees, animals and the Earth Being). Thank all animals. Thank Mother Earth for nurturing you and nurturing all beings and all life.

Then slowly come back and breathe in your heart, in your body and space. Gently come back in your present physical environment. Breathe through your whole body. Direct your consciousness with your breathing under your feet and experience your bond with the Earth Being. Breathe in your heart with gratitude, and open your eyes when you are ready to do so.

I am offering a few guidelines and suggestions for how you may wish to play in your sacred space, empower your prayers, and the energetic awareness of your divine presence.

From your Sanctuary, you have opened a sacred space of creative energies forever expanding. Your soul's divine qualities unfold and manifest in love. Your sacred sanctuary is offering the ideal place and space to learn surrendering— feeling completely safe. You are learning to embrace higher frequencies—you are learning to embrace light. With time, you will learn to hold a sacred space of peace love light all day long! Practice and learn to create joy!

Complete surrender occurs when you are free from all feelings of struggle, resentment, and judgment—when blissful serenity and joy become your way of life. The journey within your sacred sanctuary supports that experience.

When you choose to surrender and trust, you are allowing a space for the divine creative cosmic love life force energies to work for you, to flow through you, and to be revealed within you and around you. Living in your unified heart, the heart of the soul, you are free from doubts, and gratitude becomes your way of life.

> *I move with the flow of life, trusting and forever stepping in the flow of love.*

Once you surrender, you naturally open the doorway to know the consciousness of the heart—the consciousness of your soul. Your heart is forever in divine synergy and oneness with the heart of all hearts, the heart of Creation. It is the heart of God—the heart of the Creator or Source.

Meditate on these words and ask to receive the experience:

I invite and live the experience of the heart of God in the sacredness of my heart—pervading my whole beingness.
I ask to be gently guided to that experience within God's light. Thank you Father Mother God.
I choose to live anchored in the holiness of my heart. I experience the Divine Presence within me. I am surrendering, trusting, allowing, creating, and manifesting in love.

In order to create and allow peace on Earth, we have to believe in our hearts that it is possible. Peace has to be our prayer and consciousness.

CHAPTER TWO

How to be Free from Guilt, Blame, Judgment,
Jealousy, Animosity, and Resentment •
The Bliss to Forgive • Compassion •
Wishing Love, Joy, Wellness,
and Goodness to Every Being

EVERY HUMAN BEING IS NATURALLY looking for forgiveness—
consciously or unconsciously. We are naturally on a quest for love
and freedom. This inner quest for forgiveness comes from a profound and
intrinsic knowing of our divinity, a place of love within that is untouched
and forever pure—that this is lived consciously or not—it just is.

When we do not forgive, we hold on to fears, pain, resentments,
and anger. The ego is taking control, and we are temporarily not aware
of who we are. We are not living in consciousness. We are holding on
to an illusory state that creates all sorts of painful feelings.

Blaming, holding grudges, animosity, judgment, and guilt are overall
energies associated with fears. When we forgive and are compassionate,
we become conscious. All fears are transmuted into love vibrations.

Pain comes from the separation with one's Self—a holy place of love within, which is untouched. When we ignore our divine Self, we are in emotional pain.

Since the heart is programmed with divine love consciousness, we are naturally yearning to experience the nature of our true essence. That love is embedded at the source of our being—whether or not we are aware of it.

These insights are guiding you to step out from a negative matrix to be free from illusory feelings that are infringing upon harmony, happiness, and a consciousness of your true Self.

Peace is Your Natural Way to Be

We all are naturally looking for ways to be free from guilt and free from our mistakes—or what we call mistakes. In reality, there are no mistakes. Consciously or unconsciously, we are naturally looking for ways to be at peace with all life and with our Self since our essence is of pure love, divine, holy, and of God. It is necessary to learn ways to break free from negative self-punishing patterns, which blur our senses and bind us with ignorance and suffering.

As we are reaching for forgiveness, we understand that we have always been forgiven and there has never been anything to forgive— since our essence is of pure love light consciousness. We can choose to live in peace love consciousness any moment, and forgiveness takes place naturally.

When we do not forgive, we deny our very own identity. We suffer, feel fear, and despair, searching for identifications and patterns that are feeding the ego. These are illusory beliefs, illusory materialistic fixations, and addictions.

We have the ability to respond to life with consciousness. We have choices and make choices—consciously or unconsciously.

Denying or ignoring the nature of your essence is moving away from truth—from who you are—and life gets increasingly more painful. Life always brings forth opportunities to embrace your true identity and oneness—pay attention!

If you dwell on negative feelings, ignoring who you are, pain takes over. It is like digging a hole and moving deeper in that hole. It gets darker and darker—and you feel increasingly more lost and alone.

Cosmic divine consciousness—God sees you only as pure love, perfected consciousness, and whole; therefore, you are already free from all condemnations and limitations.
Recognizing your holiness is your natural way to be. It alleviates all fear, guilt, condemnation, and doubt, liberating all shadows of aloneness and uncertainty.

It Feels Good to Forgive

Every human being seeks forgiveness consciously or unconsciously. In order to experience forgiveness, all we need to do is to open our hearts and align our vibrations with our essence—it is pure love frequency. We are naturally on a quest for that love and freedom. When we forgive, we become a blessing to all life, wishing love, joy, wellness, and goodness to every being. The abundance of love, goodness, and wellness is activated and expands without limits.

It feels good to reconcile with life. It feels good to forgive and let go. Forgive yourself about any issue that is troubling you or causing you pain. Embrace your whole Self with limitless compassion. Find ways to be compassionate toward all of who you are as well as toward all beings. Stay in your heart and learn to soften your energy with love.

When you bring forth feelings of compassion, it opens the heart, guiding you to forgive. Compassion always opens the heart and moves you to high levels of love consciousness, truth, and awareness.

Embrace the realization that the spirit within you is of God, divine and of absolute perfection, harmonious, whole, and of pure love consciousness. This is who you are.

Forgive everyone who has caused you harm and pain. Make peace with all beings and with all of life. Forgive yourself and connect with the divine presence of peace within you. Free yourself from all resentments, guilt, judgment, and condemnation.
As long as you have not made peace with all of life, you are empowering energetic illusory resistances, keeping you from experiencing your wholeness and your inherent oneness with Source.

Forgiving is about shifting matrix. It is to completely move from one illusory matrix born from the ego into the matrix of true love consciousness, emanating from all life.
Forgiving is reprogramming a frequency through the power of the heart. No further judgments, resentments or animosity can take place. You are free—you have let go of controlling others and the world.
When you wish to control your world and others, you are losing your power and joy of living. When you let go of control, you are free. The qualities of love and honoring become your consciousness.

Forgiving is letting go of control and naturally awakening to compassion. Compassion is a state of awareness, understanding, and infinite grace. In compassion, you are unconditionally loving. You are living and loving from the heart—you are experiencing oneness.

Your motivation to forgive and let go of all resentments, blame, guilt, and condemnation is born from an inner longing for the personality to be completely in alignment with a consciousness of the God-Self. It is allowing God's qualities to be revealed from within. It is allowing the Tree of Life to come forward from within to exude beauty and boundless love. It is inviting an experience of God.

If you are unable to forgive, you are in pain and possibly depressed. Life becomes a struggle. Make a list of the people you wish to forgive. *Speak audibly: I ask for all energies that are not from God's realm within me and in my space, between myself and [insert the names of the people you wish to forgive] to be released into the divine light of God, on all levels, in all time, space, and dimensions, from the beginning of time to the present.*
This prayer helps clearing your mind and space.
I ask for God's peace, love, and light force energies to be awakened from within me and to flow through me, expanding in all time, space, and dimensions, between myself and [insert the names of the people you wish to forgive] from the beginning of time to the present.
See the people smiling at you and embraced by God's light. See yourself in your space smiling at them and bathing in God's light. Express gratitude to them, your divine guidance team, to life, and to God. *Thank you, God. And so it is.*

Experience your prayers in your heart as a meditation. Having such dialogues activates and supports the shift you are wishing for.

The following is another prayer intended to activate the process of forgiveness:
I choose to live in the true consciousness of my being in love, in bliss, in joy.
God's peace love light permeates my whole being and consciousness.
I invite love and goodness to be expressed in my life.
I choose peace, love, harmony, joy, and compassion as my true state of being.
I forgive myself, right now and completely. I forgive [fill-in the name/s] and all the beings, I know and I have known from the beginning of time to the present.
With love and in love, I forgive [fill-in the name/s].
I am releasing all pain and negative feelings associated with [fill-in the name/s]—into the divine light of God now and forever.
I am standing in my space within God's light and [fill-in the name/s], you are standing in your space within God's light.

I am asking that all energies, which are not of love, within me and in my space, between myself and [fill-in the name/s], be now 100 percent released into the divine light of God, in all time, space, and dimension, now and forever, and on all levels of existence. I am asking that all these spaces be filled with God's boundless love, peace, and supreme light. I am allowing and inviting goodness and wellness to be revealed and expressed. Thank you God. And so it is.

Moving from forgiveness to compassion and love leads to a new reality where you can actually imagine being reborn into true consciousness, cognizant of unlimited, divine, creative potential and infinite qualities of love.

When you are in compassion, you have forgiven since compassion is of true consciousness and bliss.

Forgive all beings and all of life to know true freedom and your God-Self.

Forgiving is a place of complete liberation and empowerment, leading to well-being and joy!

You Have a Choice

Are you tired of constantly feeling sorry for yourself? Forgive!
Are you wishing for harmony and happiness! Get motivated! Let go!

Are you tired of the struggle, guilt, resentments, pain, and fear? This energetic package has been created by the mind—multitudes of thoughts encouraged by the ego. None of it is real.

Take responsibility for your feelings. You have the awareness and ability to respond to life with love and reverence.

There are people on the planet who are not aware that they have a choice. They have been indoctrinated with negative, destructive beliefs, guilt, anger, and fears since childhood. Such circumstances and patterns are often the cause of on going conflicts, wars, genocide, terrorism, hunger, and illness.

From a place of unconditional love, you can help people to awaken to their ability and awareness to choose love—to respond to life with love.

As more people are awakening to their God-Self and true consciousness, the power of love activates people's hearts globally, in furtherance of peace on Earth.

When you live in true consciousness, you naturally negate all energetic frequencies sourcing from global and personal thought forms, empowered by the ego.

If someone's behavior is hurting you, instead of becoming resentful toward the person, look into the origin of this pain within you. Release this person into the light of God and forgive. If you feel that you have to speak your truth to resolve a situation, do it without hate or anger—speak from your heart in peace. You can do that without contacting the person. Write about it and then look within you where you need healing and nurturing love. Learn to love yourself.

If you cannot let go of the anger, close your eyes and feel this anger (for a couple of minutes) within you—try to remember when this anger really started. This anger represents a deep pain—may be from your childhood. When you remember the starting point or cause of this pain, you are then able to proceed with a deep healing. Use a few of the prayers and meditations presented in this book or any other prayer you are guided to express and use. Find peace.

Observe your thoughts and feelings. Write them down. This is an opportunity to move closer to God, to let go, and forgive. Forgive this person, and then forgive yourself. When you "forgive" you heal yourself—you clear or purify your space and consciousness—you come back to your true Self.

In which way has this experience enriched your life? Write about it.

Wisdom comes when you are ready to learn from pain. Pain is then transformed into knowledge and wisdom.

As you understand the origin of the pain, you are acknowledging it as a witness. It becomes easier to let go and release such energy. Understand that you are not the issue or the pain—and you are not the thoughts. Do not judge anything.

You are beautiful, compassionate, loving, and divine! Embrace the lesson and wisdom born from the experience, and help others through their challenges to see their true identity and light.

If you dwell on resentments, you are creating a space of suffering for yourself and for the world. When the ego takes over you are losing true consciousness and all experience of your true identity.

It is good to become conscious of all feelings of guilt, blame, jealousy, resentment, and judgment. It gives you the opportunity to recognize them separated from your true Self. Release them into the light of God. Discover the knowledge and wisdom born from the experience.

Look for the gifts of wisdom, generating increasing goodness into your life.

All of life benefits from your wisdom and love. You always have a choice of how you respond to life.

If you find yourself in a situation where you are experiencing chaos, the best decision is to move away from that situation. Create a space to receive clarity and healing. If you are unable to move away, seek spiritual counseling and help right away. You will receive help—if this is what you are wishing for in your heart. We are always guided to receive guidance and support when we open the heart to receive—and have faith despite anything! Take action! Allow and invite life to nurture you. Faith and hope open doorways of love and light in the most surprising ways.

Feel the power of the following words deep in your heart and repeat them as often as you wish:

I know my divine source and I choose to forgive now.

I choose compassion. I choose love.
I am walking in the freedom of the light on all levels, in all
time, space, and dimension of my being and life, now and
forever.
Love is my true consciousness.
I am honoring the true essence of my being.
Love is a consciousness living in me boundlessly and
manifesting in all aspects of my life. And so it is.

If you forgive and pray with strong intent from the heart, you harmonize all situations and all relationships—even if you never see the people you forgive again. It is not necessary to meet the people personally to restore a sense of serenity in the relationship. You can be free and feel free. In freeing yourself, you free them too. There is no separation.

If necessary, repeat your prayers for several days until you feel a shift. It will reach your subconscious and reprogram your cells, and DNA/RNA to higher levels of consciousness, allowing love light flow.

Every time you forgive and choose love, your light becomes brighter, more of your divinity is revealed, and more peace prevails on Earth.

If you are able to feel compassion and love for all people—even the ones you have resented—you will move toward a higher place of consciousness, contributing to harmony and peace.

Since all is energy, the nature of our experience is greatly influenced by the extent of love energies we are willing to embrace in every moment.
Do not judge the paths that others choose. Move on. We are all in God's hands, and we are of God.

In forgiveness, true consciousness is revealed and you will know only love.

UNDERSTANDING GUILT, BLAME, JUDGMENT, ANIMOSITY, AND RESENTMENT

If you feel and experience guilt, blame, judgment, condemnation, animosity, or resentment, and you are unable to move on, ask your Higher Self and divine guidance team to assist you understanding these feelings and to let go of them. Every day, take time to connect with your divine Self—focus on the breath and meditate.

Negative feelings are usually associated with fears—illusory beliefs and feelings of not being lovable and loved, of not being good enough, and of not being appreciated. These are feelings of despair and of lacking. This is all in your mind; none of it is real. None of this belongs to you, but it feels real because you are allowing the ego to be in charge of your life. You have identified with all of this. You have come to believe that all of this is you! Can you see how much power you have given to something that is not real?

If you allow your thoughts and beliefs to be in charge, you are experiencing confusion and pain, forgetting about living in the true consciousness of your essence with all its divine gifts. These gifts encompass boundless possibilities and potentialities within your consciousness and life.

When the ego is in charge of your life, you feel pain—you feel disconnected.

Learn to be aware of your ego and thoughts. Learn to sustain true awareness of your Self. Learn to use your thoughts to serve the highest purposes—use your mind to spread goodness! When the personality is thereby transcended and unites with the heart, it can be expressed from true consciousness.

When you discover the essence of love intrinsic to all life and within you, all illusions of fear associated with lack and aloneness dissipate.

If you experience animosity, jealousy, or envy, you have to snap out of that illusion! Negative feelings are covering up wounds, often from your childhood—often feeling unloved or abandoned. With awareness, reconnect with the wounded child within you, releasing all pain and filling that space with God's love. Know that you are loved and that God and life love you. Learn to love "you". Meditate and connect within with your true identity—with the beauty of your being.

Strategize and write about how you wish to bring forth increasing love, goodness, wellness, and joy in you and in your world. Every day, take positive and constructive actions from a heart-soul consciousness, trusting and surrendering.

Build your body of light in love-consciousness. Give your life to God so that his will is revealed in your life's purpose and through all aspects and expressions of your Beingness. Immerse in God's love, inviting your divine creative path to unfold harmoniously from within by living in your truth.

Negative feelings can come up in many forms and situations. If you are unable to let go of them, face these feelings and make the effort to look for their cause and source. Close your eyes and move your consciousness within. Try to understand the source of these feelings. You will find that you might be holding on to beliefs such as "I cannot" or "I am not good enough," or "I will never have," or "I don't have enough," or "this is impossible," or other similar feelings and beliefs. They represent unresolved fears and pain.

Are these feelings and beliefs serving any purpose in your life? Do you wish to continue dragging them along? Do you realize that they are illusory? Do you see how they are limiting you, in all aspects of your existence, blocking the flow of wellness and joy? Come into the realization that they are not "you". Decide to let them go and release them into the divine light of God. Choose to love all of who you are and nurture all of who you are. Breathe in all qualities of compassion, reverence, and love and breathe out all the pain to let go—and until you breathe merely love and serenity. Experience the release and feel gratitude in your heart.

Resentments are feelings of animosity and anger. They represent fear. You may feel offended and hurt. You might be resenting the world and people's behaviors. You might be judging them as cruel or hurtful. As you choose to be aware of your judgments and resentments, see how the ego—in the form of your thoughts and in your mind—has taken over your vision, perception, and your life! Become aware of the ego and understand it. Realize the power of the thoughts and what it has done to you and your life! What has it done to the world? Do you wish to contribute in this world from true consciousness to bring forth goodness, love, and joy?

Have you become what you have been resenting? Are you dwelling on what you have been resenting? This is what the ego does. It keeps you trapped in a loop, lowering your vibrations to such a level that you lose all awareness of what is real and intrinsic to all life. You know this is not what you wish to do or be. You have the choice and the ability to be free right now. You are learning to be conscious!

People's hurtful behaviors come from fear and deep pain, blocking the ability to love and feel love. It is a lack of awareness and communion with their God-Self. It is a painful place to be. Sometimes, this is the only way people know how to express pain. Throughout this book, I offer prayers and guidelines to help anyone to be free of such deep pain. **It is important to be aware without judging anything.** Judging creates deep pain and emphasizes all illusory aspects of life.

There is grace beneath all suffering—look for that grace! Let go of all that is not serving you and all that does not belong to you.

Practice forgiveness, poise, reverence, compassion, and equanimity. Love all of life! Choose to see everyone's holiness. Uplift the world with your love. Meditate and learn to breathe in the divine consciousness of your presence.

When you suffer emotionally, pay attention to your feelings and your thoughts. Learn to recognize the ego. Learn about awareness. Let go completely. Spend time in inner contemplation and spiritual practices.
Meditate and focus on the breath. You are the breath of life. Reconnect with the energy of love emanating from your essence. Through inner contemplation, the ego naturally dissipates, allowing serenity, awareness, love, and joy to nurture you and to guide you.

Guilt, blame, judgment, animosity, and resentment are created by the thoughts. All these feelings are not real. These painful feelings do not belong to you. You can drop them anytime you wish; you will then find love and purpose in your life.

When pain comes up, it is an opportunity to move closer to God. Look for the lesson and the wisdom sourcing from the experience and move into an awareness of your true Self, which is of love and joy.

Look for the lesson in what has triggered painful feelings. Instead of condemning yourself, choose to learn from your experiences. Use that lesson to improve your life—to love yourself and all beings even more. Your heart will be filled with compassion. Talk to yourself in comforting, nurturing, and loving ways. You have the ability to choose love right now. Look with gratitude at the wisdom and awareness you have received from your experiences. Do not judge; choose to receive, expand, and learn with grace. Learn to see who you truly are now!

Life is fluid light energy in motion, forever in creative transcendence and action. Light is a frequency of pure love. As you express your amazing light you have the ability to create anew in every moment from a high frequency.

Your light is your authentic Self.

UPLIFT YOUR VIBRATIONS • LEARN TO BE NURTURING

Releasing resentment, blame, judgment, jealousy, and guilt liberates you from issues that might have bound you energetically to some people with similar energies and to unpleasant situations. Releasing brings forth harmonic alignment with your true divine nature, with all beings and all of life. You feel light and free.

If you feel deeply wounded and you don't know how to get free from the pain, take several deep breaths and tell yourself that you are going to take care of this with kindness, no matter what. Trust that life is guiding you to be free. This is what life does when we are ready to find ourselves and see who we are.

It is necessary that your healing is gentle and loving. During the releasing process, it is important to never repress your feelings and pain. By allowing your feelings to surface, you are able to embrace with love the part of you that has been wounded. Expressing deep, loving compassion toward yourself is healing you now.

Truly forgive yourself.

I am ready to let go of this. I see that it does not serve any good purpose for me, for anyone else, and the world, to continue holding on to this pain. I understand that it is not mine. I forgive myself completely, and I let go now. I wish to be free, and I am free now. I now know that no pain belongs to me and is a part of me, and is a part of anyone or anything. I am of love joy consciousness, and this is where I choose now to breathe and live. I am grateful to see truth and to be a child of God. Love is my path, now and always!

You are in reality endlessly nurtured by all of life! When you surrender and have faith, you allow nurturing support to manifest into your life.

You are nurturing when you care for yourself and others with love—when you respond lovingly to life; when you choose positive thinking and positive actions; when you enjoy spending time in nature; when you choose a healthy diet; when you choose to connect with your spiritual Self in prayer and meditation; when you practice yoga; when you smile at someone; when you help someone; when you play with your dog; when you rescue animals; when you live your purpose; when you live loving life and all beings. You are nurturing when you trust life to support your soul's calling and when you choose to use your gifts in service. You are nurturing when you are grateful and appreciative. Any positive step carries you closer to awareness, joy, and freedom. Praise all of life!

You have been bestowed with unique gifts. You have the ability to use these gifts to be of service to others in beautiful ways. Nurture these gifts—honor all expressions of your Self.

Freedom Comes When We Take Responsibility

Do not blame others for your pain and misfortune. Do not blame yourself. Every time you blame someone, you are creating a negative link of energy in your space that is not beneficial in your life. Blaming yourself is only going to take you away from your true identity, balance, and joy, lessening your life force energy. Stop feeling sorry for yourself; take positive actions. Seek ways to forgive and act according to your highest soul-heart purpose. Listen to your heart.

Take responsibility for your behaviors, thoughts, and experiences. When you take responsibility, you pay attention to what you choose to create in any moment. You are then moving into greater awareness, learning to live with and in consciousness.

You have the ability to decide about the nature of the vibration you emanate. The nature of your experience is defined by the way you respond to the world and to all life, and by the quality and depth of your heart awareness—by the extent of peace love light you are allowing and inviting. This is a good example of exercising free will. Choose high energies of love—shine your light.

It is within you that your reality and experience start. No matter what has happened to you or is happening to you, take responsibility now. Move into your true power now—live from your heart.

When the people you are attracting in your life are unintentionally triggering, within you, issues you have not addressed, healed, and released, look at these feelings. People mirror your issues—they also mirror your qualities of love. Pay attention to the energies you are experiencing, and release into the light all that is not of love, honoring, and joy.
Again, take responsibility for your pain and unresolved issues, and do not blame or judge others. Blaming or judging others takes you further away from your true Self, peace, and happiness. Take responsibility and proceed with inner work.

You will attract people and situations, making you aware of your issues over and over again, until you decide to do something about these issues. We are mirrors to one another, and we project energy frequencies. We attract situations and people who match the nature of our frequencies. Your issues are about you. Do not blame, judge, or resent anyone or anything. Learn to make the appropriate changes within you in order to find clarity and peace. Choose to be nurturing and discover the consciousness of your quintessence. It is a frequency that is untouched and of pure love.

FORGIVE THE PAST

If you are holding on to pain, fear, guilt, remorse, and regrets from the past, you are blocking a flow of goodness and happiness. You are losing a considerable amount of life force and opportunities to flourish in every moment.
If you are unable to let go of the past, proceed with the following exercise. See if it activates a shift in you to be completely free from the past.

Move to the core of your past issues (the ones that have been haunting you) to understand them, feel them, and experience them. When they are completely in your face, separate yourself from the feelings. Say, *I release these issues into the light of God, now and always.* Become the observer as if you were watching a movie. By being the observer, you can now realize that you are not these issues and thoughts. They are outside of "you"—they have never touched your true identity, the divine essence of your being.

When you face your issues, you have the ability to let them go forever. Look into the sky and place them on a beautiful white cloud— and give them to the Creator.
I release all these issues and energies into the light of God. I choose to rest in God's love.

If you need additional help, blow all these painful feelings into a balloon. Breathe in love and breathe out all the pain into the balloon. Pop the balloon and say, *I let go of all energies that do not belong to me. I give all to God, to Source, to the Creator, knowing that all is transmuted into love.*
I breathe love light and blissful serenity.

The past is gone. In the present, you are free to experience your true divine identity.

> *Right now, I am liberated. I rejoice in the presence and awareness of my God-Self. I am grateful to be lovingly supported by life. I know who I am.*

Everything is of fluid light energy forever transforming and transmuting. Live from your heart so that your willingness and intentions source from a place of love and trust.

> *In peace—I allow myself to let go and be free of the past. I am moving into a consciousness of the now with gratitude and love in my heart. I choose to see and live the divine being I am.*

*I see divinity in all beings. I am loved. I am love. I am
well and safe in my space, bathing in the light of God. I am
radiating light.
I am experiencing every moment in sacredness and goodness.*

All beings with whom you have connected throughout your life
have in some way contributed to your growth. We always learn from
one another. We are teachers and students.

Everything that has happened in your life is serving a higher
purpose. It is through your life experiences that your have developed
compassion, wisdom, and awareness. Life is always leading you to
embrace more love—you know this if you pay attention!
Be grateful for all the wisdom you have received from your experiences—
this is the gift of your past. Decide that the past has no longer negative
power over your experiences and choices.
Your life's lessons are serving your highest best and the highest best of
all life.

Foster gratitude for all your blessings and for the gifts of life.

*The past has left me beautiful whispers of wisdom.
I choose love and gratitude.*

*I choose to be liberated from the past.
I welcome a consciousness of my divine presence.
I choose to experience God consciousness—my God-Self.*

THE POWER TO TRANSFORM AND UPLIFT
ANY SITUATION • CHOOSE COMPASSION

As you learn to be free from feelings of condemnation, blame, jealousy,
guilt, resentments, animosity, and judgment, you also develop in your
heart compassion and the wish to help others. Altruistic choices increase
your vital strength and joy of living. It is an energy expressed throughout

all aspect of your beingness and life. When you devote yourself to the well-being of others and the animals, when you wish to be of service, you are inviting the power of peace love light to be expressed in your life. You are living from the heart.

Perpetuating goodness, wellness, and harmony activates a flow of love.

Practice compassion toward yourself and others. Compassion is a force of love.

You have the gift and power to transform, uplift, and harmonize energies and situations by allowing love's flow.

Connect within to know truth, so that you may uplift all of life from that truth.

Any challenging situation is an opportunity to increase your consciousness of love and to love even more, guiding you closer to your God-Self. You have the ability to transform any situation to serve life's highest purpose and to look for the gift of wisdom. You have within you the ability to transform energies. Love and nurture all levels and aspects of your being and life.

Harmonizing process and prayer (to resolve challenging situations):
Write a list of your painful feelings and the names of all the people associated with these feelings. Create a sacred space and ask to bathe in God's love consciousness and supreme light. Invite everyone and everything involved in that sacred space. Write and say: Now, in this moment, I choose to forgive myself and all of life. I let go of this situation and these feelings [describe them] … I let go and I forgive … [write your list of people] … now and forever, in all time, space, and dimension. Everyone is set free. I take responsibility for my life, my experience, and my actions. I choose love and compassion. I now choose to live in peace. All life is loving.

Next to your written prayer, display a little light. Choose to place a new flower or a new crystal, or both, next to your list every day and until you feel complete serenity and love.

In the evening, before you fall asleep, go to Source and ask for divine guidance and assistance with the following prayer and visualization:
Ask to be held within God's heart, and breathe the love and light of God all around you and moving through your being.
Breathe in your heart God's love and light.
Invite your Higher Self to visit every person you wish to make peace with, holding the intention to forgive. From your heart to their heart, ask every person for the permission to connect with them in honoring—this is to show that you are acknowledging them in love and from the heart. Love opens all doors in reverence. In your mind, offer them a flower or a glowing crystal.

If you need to forgive yourself about anything—to find peace—proceed with the same prayer. The flower or crystal is for you. It is a loving reconciliation with your beautiful Self, opening your heart to experience God's love.

Proceed further with the following visualization and prayer with every person you wish to forgive. As you are getting ready to meet with this person, see yourself in a beautiful sphere of radiant sparkling white and pink light energy and then see the flower or the crystal you are holding becoming bright and radiant.

You feel so safe, loved, and nurtured in your sacred space infused with God's love and light.
You know that nothing can enter your space other that God's love.
You are now ready to visit with every person you would like to forgive and make peace with.
Bring each of them an amazing, bright, glowing flower or crystal of your choice.
Call in the violet flame to assist in the purifying and harmonizing process—to embrace you and everyone in any situation that needs to be resolved and harmonized.
The light of the flower or crystal becomes brighter and brighter as you approach the person you wish to forgive.
See this radiant light embracing you. You are now bathing in this radiant light. And as you hand him/her/them the glowing flower or the glowing crystal, this bright glowing light is embracing them completely.

Smile and see him/her/them smiling back.
Leave them in their radiant light with their magnificent glowing flower or crystal.
As you leave them, you still bathe in the radiant light.
You know that they are now embraced by God's blissful love light in their sacred space. You are in your own sacred space, in your beautiful radiance, in peace, and bathing in God's light.

If you wish, you can ask your Higher Self, God, and your divine guidance team, with the Archangels, to lead you through this harmonization process while you are asleep.
Ask that the healing and harmonization be done from God, through God, and within God's light. This harmonizing process is a beautiful way to bring forth your ability to forgive, make peace to see God in all beings, and embrace your God-Self. You have the ability to do divine work while you sleep. Your soul works in many dimensions of light while you sleep. Practice and ask for what you wish to create. Use your amazing power of intention.
Witness the beautiful outcome of this prayer in the coming days and weeks. Repeat the prayer until you actually experience the shift. The experience is lived from your heart.

You can use this prayer to harmonize any situation. Trust that this shift is serving everyone's highest purpose since life responds naturally to light and love frequencies in a way that is always guiding everyone closer to God and to love.

Sometimes, painful issues are connected to karmic issues, which can be deep wounds. Some karmic issues require to be addressed appropriately with the gentle loving guidance of a certified spiritual practitioner. Karmic issues may affect your relationships, your work, your health, or some other aspects of your life. Do not wait to seek guidance; you don't need to live in pain. When you are ready to heal and let go, you will naturally do what it takes to let go and be free from pain. You will not allow pain to affect you physically, emotionally, or in any other way. You will naturally want to seek guidance right away. You are not alone—there is help, always.

It is possible to release karmic issues without the help of a practitioner—when the soul is ready to let go. Since we are globally moving toward higher dimensions of the light, we are all naturally releasing energies that are not serving us any longer. Today, it is easy to reprogram the cells, DNA/RNA by opening our hearts through willingness, choosing compassion, honoring, reverence, gratitude, faith, and love. These prayers are guiding you to be free to love "you" and to love all beings.

All human beings have now access to high dimensions of light, allowing their light to shine and expressing their gifts in service. It is now more than ever a conscious choice available to us, to live within these high dimensions of light, to serve all of life, bringing forth peace and harmony for all beings and all life.
When you meditate, you learn to connect with the divine presence of God within you and within all creation. Within that high frequency of love light you are naturally releasing energies that are not yours. It is then possible to see who you are.

Your wisdom, compassion, and awareness are changing your life and the world. Forces of love are opening doorways of light. You are living from a synergy of love.

Compassionate love is a bridge of the heart to world peace—be the bridge!

Honoring "You" and Every Human Being

Learn to live as a conscious being, honoring you, all beings, and honoring all life. When you are able to rejoice in other people's well-being, success, and good fortune, you are able to experience that same flow. You are then living as a bright light and a blessing for all beings. Wish goodness and wellness to everyone on your path.

Dwelling on destructive or hurtful behaviors directed toward you or others is a form of violence. The personality is blinded by the ego.

The ego is in charge. In this state, you have not yet realized the essence of love within you, emanating from all beings, and from all of life. Any form of violence has ripple effects globally and energetically. They create mental, emotional, and physical misery, as well as warfare, starvation, and diseases. Pay attention to what is going on in you, with you, and in your life!

If you know people who are in deep pain and are unable to open their hearts, know that they will do so when they are ready. Honor their journey. See them embraced by God's love and light—with great compassion. See them in a good place and happy. Ask for all the archangels and masters of light to surround them and hold them in love. Prayers of compassion are powerful—your vision is powerful love. They will receive that beautiful energy.

Every human being is divinely guided and endlessly learning—and you are too. When you are not in judgment, you are honoring everyone's path and your own path. You then contribute to peace. Honoring and reverence activate the awakening of love within every being's heart.

Since every individual has free will, you cannot change anyone's beliefs and choices. But by raising your vibrations in compassion and love, you will naturally help bring forth these energies in all beings to various degrees—according to their own inner choices of consciousness. When you choose to emanate high frequencies of love, everyone receives love, including the Earth Being and all of creation! Love all beings.

I rejoice in everyone's good fortune, happiness, and well-being.

When your light shines, there is a ripple effect, activating more of these frequencies around the world and contributing to increasing peace and harmony. "Peace love light" knows no limit—it is the essence of life forever embracing you and loving you.

Prayer for Trust and Serenity

I choose to live in the peace emanating from the core of my being—knowing that I always choose to do my best in the moment, living from my heart, and allowing the power of love light to lead my path. I surrender with ease and breathe in the divine consciousness of love light sourcing from all that is—and sourcing from the one heart of God. I am now free, bathing in divine cosmic consciousness and guided by a higher power of love— it is God's love.

My past has left me with boundless gifts of wisdom. I am grateful and at peace with my past. I am at peace with all beings and all of life. In every moment, I breathe in the consciousness of my divine presence, and the love in all life.

I am on a new path of consciousness—one that is of love, uplifting, and enlightening, and one that is in alignment with all qualities of God.

I have wonderful ideas, and I draw wonderful opportunities to bring forth positive actions and synergies in my surroundings and in the world—always contributing to increasing goodness, wellness, beauty, and love.

I choose to see the highest good in all beings and in all life. I choose love, reverence, and compassion.

Every day, I am joyfully awakening to the awareness of my sacredness and light—and the sacredness and light in all life. I move with the flow of life with ease and peace, allowing love divine consciousness to guide my life.

I allow my new path to unfold gently, in harmony and love. I feel the joy! I am safe, nurtured, supported, and guided by all of life.

God loves me.
I take action listening to the consciousness of my heart, forever
honoring all beings.

I experience unconditional love for all beings and for me.
I see the presence of God's love in all beings, everywhere,
and in me.
Mother Earth loves me and nurtures me.
I love and honor the Earth Being and bask in its beauty.
My heart is filled with boundless gratitude.

Feel and experience the energy of this prayer, the energy of the words in your heart, in your whole being, and in your life.

As you open the space for God's love to work with you and through you, you feel love from all beings, wishing goodness and wellness to everyone. You are allowing your light to shine. Your divine Self is free to express all qualities of love. You naturally stop reacting to the vicissitude of life since your vibrational frequency has reached high energies of love and awareness. You are living in consciousness.

All is of God. All is love. The presence of God is in everyone
and in everything, omnipresent. Love light harmonic synergy
is the nature of the life force sourcing from all of creation.
All life is a sempiternal creative energetic matrix of God's
love, light, beauty, bliss, grace, joy, and infinite holy
qualities—also present within the Tree of Life.

I choose to dance in a synergy of peace love light frequency.
I choose to live, dance, and breathe in the frequency and
consciousness of my spiritual essence.
I now gladly embrace the freedom of my soul!
I rejoice in a delightful serene Presence within me. It is a
frequency of boundless love.
I am honoring the consciousness of my divine presence. I am
honoring all beings in unconditional love and sacredness.

CHAPTER THREE

The Power of Thoughts, Feelings,
Emotions, Beliefs, and Words •
The Power of Gratitude, Joy, and Love

CREATE A NEW RELATIONSHIP WITH YOUR SELF

YOUR ENVIRONMENT AND EXPERIENCE REFLECT your personal inner beliefs, emotions, intentions, and thoughts.

Since all is energy, and energy is in motion and fluid, it is possible to transform any energy frequency all the way to the core of our cells, DNA, and RNA.

The physical world responds to people's choices and levels of consciousness. Our focus, our beliefs, and cellular programs are synergies reflected in our experience and our reality lived in the moment.
In every moment, we are creating a specific flow of energy emanating from our feelings, intentions, emotions, thoughts, and words. They are a reflection of how we perceive the world and how we respond to life in every moment.

Most people identify with what they have and with the way they look. For most people, the physical material world triggers a multitude of thoughts and illusory beliefs, running people's lives. A multitude of thoughts are controlling people's lives, often leading to pain, depression, or despair. People develop false perceptions when the ego rules their experience, creating a distorted view of the world.

This identification with ego, thoughts, and illusory aspects of life fade away as we enter higher dimensions of light and awaken to our true nature—when we spend time in contemplation and meditation—when we commune with the core essence of life.
Now is the time for the whole world to move into the consciousness of the heart. It is a consciousness of unity and unconditional love.

It is possible for your negative thoughts to be dissipated and to have no more influence over your life and experiences—the ego fades away, allowing the personality to be reborn in light consciousness. Thoughts are transmuted into energies of pure love consciousness. You are then experiencing a divine creative flow and blissful serenity—you discover your true divine presence and essence. It is from that place of awareness that you wish to live your life. You are then using your mind and thoughts as beautiful tools to serve higher purposes. Your mind and thoughts are magic tools to create goodness, harmony, and joy in your world.

Live in the consciousness of your true nature and identity.

If your feelings and thoughts are sourced from awareness, from the true nature of your presence, they feel empowered with love life force energy, creativity, and blissful serenity—they are of peace and joy.

The true nature of the Self emanates a bright sun shining its rays reaching all beings and all that is. It is a power of love, true knowledge, and serenity that is sempiternal and boundless. Learn to express your thoughts from that sacred place within you.

Your state of consciousness and the energy frequencies you are emanating and dwelling upon are greatly influencing the progress and process of your life. Your life experience is guided by your mental and emotional behavior—by the way you choose to respond to life.

Your thoughts, feelings, emotions, beliefs, and words reflect the way you respond to life and the way you perceive the world—they reflect your relationship with your Self.
It is in the relationship with your own Self that your life's story has its roots. Explore and understand with consciousness the nature of the relationship you have with your Self. Learn to love and honor your Self.

Too often, we forget that we are worthy, loved, and sacred beings. We don't know how to receive anymore—we forget that we are deserving of love, goodness, wellness, and happiness. Pay attention to this energy. Are you open to receive love and kindness? Are you kind to yourself?

Do you love who you are? Are you honoring all of who you are? Are you kind to your Self? Do you truly see who you are?
The nature of your relationship with your Self reflects the relationship you have with the external world and vice versa.
Is your mind trapped in a matrix of illusions, pain, and suffering?

Learn to be aware of all your feelings, emotions, thoughts, and beliefs. If necessary, write them down so that you can understand what is really going on in your life and in you. Understand that, by recognizing your patterns, you become conscious of what you are experiencing—and why. When you have an understanding of your patterns, it becomes easier to bring positive changes into your life. It is then possible to take conscious steps toward increasing wellness, harmony, and joy.

People who do not pay attention to their painful issues—in order to heal and let go of them—are increasingly controlled by their emotions and thoughts. This can sometimes escalate into self-destructive behaviors, addictions, anger, rage, violence, or profound depression.

With time, it is possible to feel completely lost. This condition creates energetic disturbances within one's being.

Such inner turmoil creates energetic gaps or openings in someone's field, inviting additional external low energies. These low vibrations can reach the physical body and create illness. When someone loses himself or herself in ongoing negative thoughts and emotions, it can create various mental and health problems. But such states and conditions are always reversible. Whatever the situation, it is always possible to heal and go back to one's divine presence to find peace, bliss, harmony, and love. One's God-Self is forever untouched and of pure love.

I emphasize the importance of paying attention to how you feel, so that you may take steps to heal and let go of painful issues. You are forever a divine being of God. It is never too late to love.

Why do we get caught up in our thoughts to the point that we identify with them? Because from thoughts come feelings and emotions. We then think that this must be what is real. Observe the relationship between your thoughts and your feelings and emotions—you have the ability to choose the nature of your thoughts and create any emotion and feeling you wish.
Choose to express all of who you are with reverence and from a consciousness of your God-Self.

Do not judge your feelings. The expression of feelings is beautiful. They are guiding you, if you pay attention to them with wisdom and awareness.

As you understand the origin of your feelings and make peace with life, see them as streams of light moving through you and opening your heart with love. You are transmuting energies and you are clearing your space.

Focus on your breathing—breathe in your heart and allow all thoughts to fade away. *I gently let go of my thoughts.* As you liberate your mind, your feelings and emotions are softened, and they are replaced by a delightful space of serenity and bliss.

Your thoughts, intentions, and feelings are energies—you have the ability to choose their nature and frequencies to better your life and the lives of others.

When you embrace the love and joy of God's divine presence, the personality-mind and heart are working together as one—liberating your true identity. Your light body awakens and shines!

In order to experience the freedom and love of your divine presence, it is necessary to clean up house. You have the ability to clear and purify your mind, bodies, and fields by completely surrendering to God and life. Invite love consciousness to guide your path, get involved in spiritual practices and studies, explore the qualities of spirituality and meditate. Learn to be nurturing and loving on all levels of your life—with "you" and with all beings.

It is important to be liberated from all thought forms of hatred, bigotry, or jalousie. Those energies are detrimental to your emotional, mental, and physical balance and health. They are polluting your world, your life, and the whole world!

The programming embedded within your cellular memory influences your life. Look for any recurring negative behaviors, feelings, or pain you don't understand and have not been able to let go. If some of your cellular programs are holding negative emotions and negative patterns, you have the ability to release them and reprogram your cellular frequencies choosing awareness, love, positive intentions and the power of your willingness—using the prayers and insights in this book—in meditation or using some of the amazing spiritual teachings available to the world today. Remember that all is fluid light energy and frequency of love at its source. This is your essence.
Meditate and delve into your spiritual practices and studies—you will experience the shift in you. You will experience a liberation of your true being!

Seek help from a certified spiritual practitioner, if you are looking for support and guidance. Do not give up. You can be free of any pain or energetic blockage the moment you commit to it from your heart.

I invite you to experience the following process: *"I breathe the peace, love, and light of God in my heart. I bathe in God's light right now. I breathe in the heart and consciousness of God right now. I call upon Father Mother God and divine assistance from the archangels, angels of light, my divine guides of light and master guides—and master healers of the light.*
I release into the light of God programs, beliefs, and behaviors that are not serving my Higher Self. God's love light consciousness permeates my cells, DNA/RNA, my mind, and consciousness, reaching all my bodies and fields."
Speak distinctly the list of the behaviors, issues, pain, and beliefs you wish to let go. "I release …[describe]… into the light of God, in all time, space, and dimensions—now and always. It is done. Thank you."
Speak distinctly the list of the positive behaviors and beliefs you wish to live from! Talk to your whole being, your mind, your cells, DNA, and RNA, (you have a close relationship with your cells). Talk to God and ask for these changes within your being. All aspects of your being have consciousness. Then say: "I am asking for all divine qualities of God to awaken from the core of my being and infuse my cells, mind, and consciousness, now and always. It is done."

For a few minutes, breathe God's love light through your whole being, in your mind, and brain, and anchor the love light in all your bodies and fields, in all your cells, all the way under your feet, and into the Earth Being. Bathe in God's love and light! Express deep gratitude. Be still and pay attention to the energies.
Repeat this process until you know the shift is happening. If you work from your heart and surrender, you will activate and experience a healing. This healing is an activation of an increasing flow of love light sourcing from the core of your being.
Breathe love light energies as you say the words. You can transform your genetic blueprint since the essence of your being is fluid light energy and frequency.

If you feel discomfort, confusion, despair, or fear, open your heart to new ways of approaching life that are gentle, honoring, and loving

so that you may open doorways to a new paradigm—the love that is inherently at the source of all creation.

Love light energy is a force of life living within you and living in your breathing.

Create a new and sacred relationship with your Self and all life. Learn to embrace the love that springs from all life.

As you choose to surrender and forgive, you clear your energy field from toxic energies—nothing is blocking your light. Your light body is activated—the Tree of Life is activated at the core of your being. The Tree of Life belongs to God's divine design and consciousness within you and within all life.

As you discover the sacredness in all life, open your heart and feel love for you, all beings, and all of creation. Learn to love and honor all of life.

Life is supporting you in infinite, loving, nurturing ways—in every moment— guiding you closer to your God-Self. Open your heart and delve into the sacredness of your being!

The roots of pain are associated with feelings of aloneness, feeling lost, feeling separated from everything and everyone—from God and your God-Self. Such pain grows if there is a lack of inner spiritual work, inner contemplation, and a lack of willingness and faith.

Where does your attention dwell? What are your intentions? How much power and truth do you bestow upon your willingness and faith?

"Loneliness is like the leprosy of the West. The biggest problem is spiritual deprivation," said Mother Theresa.

Explore your multidimensionality from a consciousness of love. Choose with awareness the nature of your attention, intentions, thoughts, words, beliefs, and feelings. Use your mind and these tools to better yourself and the world. Choose them to be a source of wisdom, compassion, and love. Uplift your feelings. The mind has to work from the heart and through the heart.

Within you are the doorways to harmony, wisdom, divine knowledge, divine creativity, compassion, happiness and love.

Nurture the qualities of loving-kindness. Your world and reality start within you. Which reality do you choose?

It is possible to become acquainted with feelings of pain or become addicted to pain without consciously knowing it. That place of pain has grown to be so familiar that it becomes difficult to imagine life without it. This is a painful place to be. It is unfortunate that there are adults and children today who have lived in war situations since they were born. It is important to express infinite compassion and send peace love light to them and their countries.

If you are this child or adult, surrender in prayer and meditation to experience the presence of God within you—a divine presence of peace and love that is infinitely blissful and forever in oneness with you—living as a holy and divine design within you.

Everyone has the ability to find peace and bliss within. It is our true nature.

Learn to be in touch with the nature of your frequencies and learn to align them with the frequencies of the heart. Your willingness, your power, and your love are sourcing from within your heart. Learn to use the power of the mind through your heart—for the goodness of all life. Learn to raise your vibrations.

Choose your thoughts, feelings, beliefs, and words from a consciousness of the heart—and use these tools to create peace and joy.

Understand Your Feelings and Emotions

Honor your feelings and emotions; they are telling you what is really happening in you, with you, and in your life. Feelings originate from thoughts and are linked to your intentions and beliefs. They are also linked to your inner cellular programs.

Write a list describing the nature of your emotions and feelings, and search how they are connected to your intentions and beliefs. Take time, even several days, to complete your list. Become aware of your focus and the thoughts you are dwelling on—they are triggering your emotions and feelings.

As you contemplate your list, look for what is triggering these feelings and emotions. Make a new list of the patterns and issues that are creating these feelings and emotions.

Contemplate your lists and decide if you wish to continue living with these patterns, issues, and feelings. Are they serving higher purposes? Do they make you happy? Are they creating pain? Are they creating joy and goodness?

As a support to invite increasing balance and peace within you, you may use the power of the breath. Breathe deeply all the way into your belly. Breathe in, peace love light and breathe out all issues, patterns, feelings, and emotions you wish to release or transform. Do this until you experience a shift within you—until you feel lighter and free. You are not these patterns, issues, feelings, and emotions—you are an amazing divine being of God. With time, your prayers and meditations are leading you deeper within the essence of your true identity—a presence of pure love.

You have the ability to activate your divine codes and realign your cellular programs with the consciousness of your God-Self, since you belong to one divine matrix and design—God's consciousness. Free the mind and choose love! As you are moving into true consciousness you are experiencing the heart and mind of God. All life is created from one source of light!

Meditate on the reality that you are a ray of golden white light infused with divine love—with God's divine qualities. Divine light and God's love frequencies are now permeating the memory of your cells, your bodies, fields, mind, and consciousness. Your cells remember! You remember who you are!
All that does not belong to you is liberated and transmuted into blissful love by the light. You are awakening your God-Self.

> *I release—with ease and grace—into the divine light of God all that does not belong to me, in all time, space, and dimensions. I am free. I choose to live within the true consciousness of my divine being—it is blissful love, joy, and serenity—and so it is.*

When we fear a situation, it is good to pay attention to this energy. It is important to find out within us why we experience this fear. Listen to your inner divine guidance by moving deep within your heart.
People who live in fear of others, give power to what they don't want, blocking all natural synergies of love light flow. It is important to learn to be infinitely forgiving, compassionate, and to open our hearts. Peace prevails on Earth when our hearts are open, loving all beings and all life.

Practice living within new frequencies of peace, compassion, reverence, and love. Revere the beauty and sacredness of life.

Write a list about how you wish to be of service—everything you wish to create—with all the qualities of love you wish to nurture and express. Listen to your heart.
During the following days, weeks, and months, complete your list with your positive affirmations and dreams. Practice experiencing the frequencies of your visions from a place of love and joy. What you focus upon becomes your life— pay attention and practice with consciousness. Live from your heart. You have the ability to change your experience.

Your true identity is a program or design embedded in the core of your inner being, a divine place of love that is forever pure and blissful— untouched by human emotions and thought forms.

I am light within the light.

Sometimes, people experience a deep void or emptiness that is often very painful. These feelings of emptiness are lived as something that is missing within. They are feelings of aloneness associated with despair. Because it is so painful, many people try to cover up these feelings with destructive behaviors and addictions to escape the pain. In reality, the pain gets deeper and deeper. These feelings of emptiness need your special loving attention.

This void or emptiness takes place when there is a lack of inner spiritual work and connectivity with Source. This void heals when it is filled with God's love— when you commune with the love sourcing from the unified heart of your divine being or higher Self, and the love sourcing from all life.
Through daily prayers and meditations, you are able to reactivate the consciousness of your God-Self.

As you sustain an inner awareness of your divine loving presence and live within that consciousness, the power of love light reflects in all aspects of your existence and personal expression, creating infinite rays of love light. Your emotions calm down and your feelings are blissful and serene.

Your Bodies Respond to Love in Harmony and with Harmony

Within your auric or energy field, all your bodies and light bodies embrace and encompass the physical body. All your bodies and the physical body respond to the nature of your thoughts, feelings, and beliefs. All your bodies and the physical body respond to your choice of consciousness.

Our bodies are known as the physical, etheric, emotional, mental, astral, etheric spiritual, celestial, and Ketheric bodies. We have additional bodies of light expanding and radiating light as we are awakening and living from the heart.

Right now all our bodies are moving into higher dimensions of light including the physical body. As we raise our vibrational frequency we receive the experience of our light bodies—if we choose to embrace the shift and open the heart. As the light bodies are activated our molecular structure is transmuting into a lighter luminescent energetic design. Now is the time to serve as emissaries of peace.

My intent is to explain what happens when we move away from love consciousness and from our divine Self. I wish to convey a clear understanding of how these energies are working in our lives.

Negative thought patterns are energetic forces in action, harming all aspects of your being. Over time, they pollute your bodies and your environment. All is energy in action, and all is one.
Perpetuating negative thought patterns and beliefs are causing blockages to the natural flow of love life force within one's being. Such low frequencies are not an energetic match to the natural vibrational essence and synergy of your being and life.

The fundamental nature of your being is in harmonic oneness with a global divine design of light patterns and synergies by which all is created. Your whole consciousness has to resonate at a high frequency of love and reverence in order to experience harmonic synergy and well-being.

If you dwell on negative destructive thought patterns for a long time, they will create serious energetic disturbances within your field, bodies, and cells. Ongoing negative thoughts cause chronic stress and fear, shattering your being and your whole energy field. This is when you lose balance and feel sick—and get sick. You are polluting your space and the Earth Being.

Destructive thought patterns lead to additional destructive behaviors. It is a state of unconsciousness. They represent forms of violence or aggression directed toward you, all beings, the Earth Being, and all life. These low frequencies are moving through all bodies all the way to the physical body, interrupting the natural flow of life force, creating psychosomatic pain, illness, and depression. Such patterns and lack of awareness may generate violent behaviors if issues are not resolved, released, and healed on time—and if the person does not connect with his or her true identity while engaging in spiritual healing, meditation, and prayer.

Negative thought form patterns are violent wave frequencies directed toward the Self, toward all beings, and the world. They invite and create what is often called "entities". In this specific occurrence, such entities represent low negative energies created and activated by energetic thought forms—feeding from people's mental misery and ego. These energies are connected to an energetic global toxic pollution, generated and sustained by "humankind ego and ignorance of the Self". People who create and invite in their space negative energetic forces are opening up to additional collective negative forces. These forces are living entities—they are powerful energies created by people's fears, mental and emotional misery, and ignorance of the God-Self.

These forces or entities can sometimes take over the personality and live within one's energy field, sometimes invading the physical body too. They play with people's minds and emotions, reinforcing the ego illusory mindset. They are energetic living forms, feeding themselves from the person's life force and the energies of despair, fear, hatred, or any other destructive pattern. They deplete one's being of vital energy flow and life force.

As a spiritual practitioner, I have come to witness that mental and emotional distress and disorders are often the reason of energetic interferences caused by entities—also hurting the physical body.

It is possible to release such energies or entities into the light of God anytime a person decides to reconcile with life and chooses to be guided by love. Everything is energy consciousness. This is why it is important to live in consciousness of our true nature and nurture lovingly all our beingness with all life. It is important to know who we are and live within that reality and truth.

If you fear, resent, or hate even one person, you are harming yourself, this person, and the world. Fear, hate, and resentment are contributing to increasing global chaos, and warfare. These frequencies are depleting one's beingness of life force and of the joy of living. You are feeding your cells and your whole being with an energy that is a poison, creating toxins and acidity in your physical body.

Thoughts, intentions, feelings, emotions, and words reflecting ongoing self-destructive, hurtful, and violent patterns create psychosomatic pain and illness. As I mentioned earlier, with time, they disrupt one's energy field, creating energetic openings or holes within the auric field (energy field) all the way to the physical body. This is when the life force within the physical body is disrupted. The physical body gets out of balance and gets sick. Through these openings or holes, people lose their life force, which engenders all kinds of illness. People become increasingly vulnerable to various negative energies, forces, and illness.

Destructive energies are created from humans' thought forms.

Thoughts, intentions, beliefs, feelings, and emotions are living forces and energetic frequencies. They attract and invite the same frequencies you are dwelling on.

You invite and emanate energetic frequencies from your decisions and choices. It is important to be aware of what you create in every moment from any expression of your being. It is learning to live with consciousness.

If you are convinced that you are a victim, the ego is in charge and the mind is trapped. Wake up and use your willingness to liberate your mind and space. Meditate, pray, and study spiritual teachings—discover who you are.

In order to receive clarity and understanding about your potential and multidimensionality, learn to live in the sacredness of the now, conscious of your divine presence. When you live in true consciousness, nothing from the external world has power over you. You live and experience a consciousness of love and harmony sourcing from all of life. You are in energetic alignment with all creation, shining your light and bathing in light.

All of life is energy frequency and synergy.

Great challenges and unexpected events can sometimes be experienced as traumatic if the person is not deeply connected with his or her God-Self—a lot of life force is lost, and one's whole being gets shattered. It is important to learn to respond to life with wisdom, reverence, and grace.

If you are losing your life force because you are fighting life, you probably experience emotional pain as if you were trapped in a deep dark hole, and you don't know how to get out of it. You are unable to see the light. Please know that there is a way out. Peace love light is right here in you, and you are bathing in it. In order to see it and experience it, you have to liberate the mind and explore the consciousness of the heart and soul.

Your daily experience sources from the inner consciousness you allow and choose—even if you are not fully aware of it in the moment.

Life offers boundless opportunities to grow, to move into further awareness and greater alignment with your divinity.
If you do not look at challenges as opportunities to move closer to God and keep fighting life, you will move deeper into suffering and struggles, inviting physical and emotional pain.

When you open your heart to love, it activates your pineal gland, your DNA, and RNA with light, connecting you to higher planes of existence that are of infinite divine intelligence, love light consciousness. All your bodies of light are activated and your whole being shines like a sun. The third eye is activated. It is the pineal gland.

The pineal gland is activated by light and by love sourcing from the heart, the core of your being. The pineal gland and the pituitary body have to vibrate in harmonic synergy to activate your body of light and light consciousness. As you let go of the struggle, the ego is softened, inviting the consciousness of the heart to awaken. You are allowing and inviting love light flow in all aspects of your being, activating the Stargate of the heart—balance and harmony are restored in all bodies and within your whole energy field. Your physical health improves greatly and your body finds harmony.

Honor all of who you are. Your joy, well-being, and health are born from the love you are allowing, expressing, giving, and embracing.

> *I choose to use my mind and my thoughts to serve higher purposes in reverence and with unconditional love.*
>
> *My mind is a gift. I use it for love and in love.*
>
> *All of my being responds to love in harmony and with harmony.*
>
> *I open my heart to receive boundless love from God, from the creation, from all life.*

THE POWER OF WORDS

The nature of your words reflects your inner consciousness—whether you are aware of it or not. Pay attention to the words you speak. If you notice that your verbiage emanates, most of the time, low vibrations, vibrations of disempowerment, resentments, insecurity, or bigotry, seek within you which issues are causing such state of mind and behaviors. Learning to be aware of your intentions, emotions, feelings, and thoughts by paying attention to your verbiage is one more way to live with increasing consciousness.

Choose words that make you feel good and reflect your higher Self with all the love and joy you are eager to give and embrace. Pay attention to the vibrational frequency of your words.
Your verbiage is reflecting your thoughts, feelings, beliefs, and consciousness. Your verbiage is reflecting your focus—attention and intention—and how you perceive life. Change the choice of your verbiage and its vibration if they are not of compassion, honoring, reverence, beauty, and joy. The energy frequency of your words is received by your whole being and is strongly felt in your physical body and emotional body. If you pay attention, you know why and when you feel good and you know why and when you feel bad.

Your choice of words is another tool you wish to use with awareness, love, compassion, and reverence to create goodness, harmony, and joy. Your magic wand is love!

Through love light energetic frequency of words, you are also able to reprogram your genetic blueprint and experience an awakening of consciousness. You can do that through prayers, visualizations, and affirmations—through meditations and mantras (sacred words repeated in meditation) and focusing on the breath.
Mantras, prayers, sounds, inner stillness, and light work invite and activate high frequencies of peace love light, allowing harmonization of the cells, bodies, and fields. They open a space inviting harmonization and activation of the energy centers or chakras. They can reach with ease the program of the cells and activate divine energetic realignment within your genetic blueprint.

Ancient Gregorian chants—or any high frequency emanating from sounds, music, and mantras, or prayers have harmonizing powers, raising one's frequencies. They also raise the frequency of the location where these sounds and words are repeated. Some languages (and words) hold higher vibrational frequencies—they are called the sacred languages. Those high frequencies extend their healing and harmonizing powers to reach all of life. Love light energy-sound knows only oneness.

Words are synergies of energies that are affecting you in a positive or negative way, also depending on the nature of the emotions you are projecting when you speak.

Become aware of the energy you are projecting in everything you speak and everything you do. Use your words in sacredness. Learn about honoring yourself and all beings by choosing consciously your verbiage.

Words are disempowering if they are not aligned with goodness, harmony, honoring, and love. They always reflect your emotions and your inner state.

Speak words that are honoring to you, all beings, and all Life. Learn about the sacred aspect of life in all that you do.

> *I am learning about the true power of love in all aspects of life. My words and intentions are honoring and loving to all life.*
>
> *I nurture within the qualities of loving-kindness, and I express these qualities in my words.*

WHICH ENERGIES ARE YOU PASSING ON TO YOUR CHILDREN?

If you have children and if you keep perpetuating thoughts of anxiety and worry—projecting the worst for their future through your fears—you will eventually pass on these fears to your children. Be aware of the energy you project and what you dwell on—you are creating an experience.

Your children often take on your personal beliefs and feelings. They are open to you, trusting you and loving you, and expect to be loved. If you fear for your children most of the time, these negative energies and thoughts are shattering the harmonic flow of infinite goodness and wellness in your life and in your children's lives too. Your children may take on these vibrations and issues since they are so open to your energies. Some children will take on more than others, according to their purpose and mission.

You have a special energetic bond with your children. It is so important that in your heart you see your children happy, knowing about their inner divine guidance and sacred path. You have to be able to do all of this for yourself first. Learn about your inner divine guidance and connect with your true Self—your divine essence. You will then have the most wonderful time with your children, experiencing the power of love and joy.

If you let go of fears and heal painful issues, you will be able to better guide your children on a path that is empowering to them and to you. They are your teachers as you are their teacher. In your heart, know that love is your guide and true power.

See and understand your children's intuitive abilities and gifts. They naturally know where to find harmony and love, and they know where there is chaos, fears, and unbalanced energies. They naturally dwell on love.
If you do not hold a loving space to honor their intuitive abilities, blinding them with fears, negative indoctrinations, and personal negative patterns, they will most likely move away from their intuitive gifts—or some of their intuitive gifts—as they grow up. You are then passing on energies, shattering their natural balance and abilities to feel supported by life, to trust life, and to express their creativity freely.

Trust life and love your children tenderly. Be aware of their gifts, oneness, and divinity. See their beauty and divinity and trust their inner guidance. See all these good things within you so that you become free.

You are then allowing your children to be who they are—guided by divine love.

It is from the heart that you connect with your children. They know and feel your consciousness. Allow them to blossom in harmony. Allow the natural expression of their true nature of joy. Living from the heart, as parents, naturally allows the best in them to be expressed, together with their creative abilities.

They will surprise you with their choices and intuitive abilities. They are very aware of what is going on around them. Your children are naturally in tune with joyous, loving, and uplifting energies. They naturally express them. High energies are natural to them and in alignment with their true nature—you have to remember this for you too.

Do not suffocate and invade your children's space with your worries, negative beliefs, and chronic fears. Take lovingly care of yourself, surrender, and trust.

As parents, step out from negative patterns and free yourself by embracing your divinity—your beautiful Self. Allow the natural energetic flow of harmony and goodness to permeate your life and being. You will then allow and create the most delightful and amazing time with your children. You will be able to love them freely—with a free mind and from the heart. All interaction with your children will emanate fun and loving energies.
Let go of the heavy energy of worries and stress you have been experiencing—if this is what you are experiencing.

Trust the process of life and make peace with life. Your children are delighted to embrace your loving and high energies since you are now allowing them to fully express love and joy in all aspects of their lives. You are holding a beautiful space of joy in your heart. Your children are blossoming, connected, and aware. They are of love and joy, expressing divine creativity. They will attract situations and people in alignment with these loving energies. They will naturally move toward what is loving and harmonious. Live in your heart—your children will then live in their hearts as they grow up. You are their teacher, and they are your teacher.

There are different types of fear. You might have felt uneasy, scared or wary about a situation that is not in alignment with love, harmony, and goodness. This type of fear is your intuition talking to you. Such intuitive feelings of fear last a short time. They come from your inner intuitive guidance. Learn to recognize your inner guidance and learn to act with wisdom. Your children are aware of energies and are intuitive. Encourage them to listen to their inner divine guidance.

When life presents its challenges, teach your children to look at every challenge in a constructive way—from a place of strength instead to feeling victimized. The positive aspects of a challenge are always the lesson and the wisdom that are given and offered by life. Look for what enriches the soul in any situation and teach your children about it. They will stay strong in life and find ways to overcome any situation. They will be able to turn situations around with wisdom, grace, and love.
Help your children understand the lessons and wisdom born from their challenges—show them how these experiences may benefit their future. Teach them about gratitude and compassion. They will grow and expand in wisdom, awareness, and so much more, embracing all gifts from life.

Children's natural ability to embrace what feels harmonious and loving is shattered when they are under the influence of negative parenting and fear-based indoctrinations.
It is never too late to reverse any situation. If you wish for this change, you have to change inside and connect with your God-Self. You have to reconcile with life and connect with Source within. Your children will receive that new energy of love. It is never too late to choose love. Forgive yourself—for "you" and for your children.

The reality of who you are is divine and pure love. By living that reality in your heart, on a soul level, you naturally allow your children to sustain the reality and awareness they are naturally born with. If you have not attended to that awareness, it is never too late to be in alignment with the sacredness of your being. Choose to sustain feelings that are comforting, compassionate, nurturing, and joyful.

You have the ability to live a healthy relationship in love and harmony with your children. When you are free, they will surprise you in the most amazing ways.

Children often feel insecure and unloved when parents are unable to be an anchor of harmony and love. Sometimes, they receive that anchor from other family members, teachers, or close friends.

Children naturally feel free to express their highest qualities and creative gifts with joy and harmony. Take that ride with them and have fun!

Divine guidance is in your children and within you. No one walks alone.

Be aware of the energies you project. Understand the multidimensionality of your beingness and the multidimensionality of your children.

Allow your children to be who they are by allowing "you" to be who you are. Embrace life with joy and all the goodness and fun you deserve with your children. It is available to you now.

Trust the process of life. Your children are experiencing everything their souls are choosing to experience—life always attends to serve their highest best according to their choices. See the beauty and blessing in it and make peace with it. From your heart, see them happy and walking in God's light. It is a way to hold sacred space. It is a sacred space for you, too. Choose goodness and love now! Choose to be happy now!

> *I choose my intentions, thoughts, and verbiage to be a vibrational extension of my God-Self—of God's consciousness living in me.*

Embrace Joy, Love, Peace, and Gratefulness

Rejoice in the good fortune and happiness of others. It is an empowering place to experience and in which to abide. Rejoicing in the good fortune of others moves you to a high frequency that is uplifting and is reflected in your thoughts, emotions, beliefs, and words. In reality, it moves your whole being into frequencies of joy— activating your light.

Criticizing other people leaves you disempowered, since the energy emanating from your words, thoughts, feelings, and emotions have low frequencies.

Holding on to negative feelings, resentments, jealousy, or hatred toward people who are successful or happy—or toward anyone in general—is destructive and disempowering. Such behaviors and frequencies greatly disrupt the harmonic flow of goodness, wellness, and harmony in your existence and on the planet.

Rejoice in other people's wellness, success, love, and abundance. Open your heart to appreciation, gratefulness, and the beauty in all creation.

How do you wish to be of service and contribute to harmony and peace?

If your focus is directed toward receiving success and wealth for selfish reasons, it will not bring the happiness you are wishing for—since you are not living your purpose. You will always feel that something is missing in your life. If you get up every morning with the intent to bring forth increasing harmony and goodness into the world, you naturally create a flow of magnetized love, abundance, and joy. In addition of your path to success and wealth or living your success and wealth, you will live your purpose and uplift people in beautiful ways. Love and goodness have a ripple effect all around the world. You are contributing to peace and harmony and you will feel whole.

Daily, look for ways to bring forth well-being, goodness, beauty, peace, and joy in you and in others—in harmony and reverence. You can bring forth these qualities in everything you do and in your work. Create happiness in you and around you. Learn to live in sacredness, honoring all life. Live your true purpose!

> *I choose my life to be a joyous adventure where I nurture all qualities of love, peace, and gratitude, honoring who I am in every moment and honoring all beings.*

Gratitude and appreciation are from the heart. They hold a powerful magnetic flow of infinite goodness.
In gratitude, you recognize the sacredness of life in every moment. It is a place of awareness and grace.

Gratefulness, expressed from the heart, holds high vibrational frequencies, activating a flow of abundance, wellness, and joy. Feeling and expressing gratefulness holds a powerful positive creative energy in all aspects of your life. When you are grateful, you connect with your true identity, anchoring you even further in the awareness of your true nature.

> *Gratitude is a vibrational frequency in alignment with my God-Self.*
> *I choose to live every moment in gratitude and appreciation, rejoicing in that energy of nurturing love.*

When you live in joy and appreciation, all qualities of love and peace are expressed. You are walking as a bright sun, activating increasing goodness, wellness, and love consciousness for all beings.

> *Within me is a divine resonance of gratitude, holding a magnetic power of calmness, joy, and grace, blessing every moment of my life with love.*
>
> *Bliss and grace are sempiternal qualities and emanations of*

God within me. They are frequencies sourcing from all life, lovingly supporting me and embracing me.

Imagine your whole being as fluid light energy. When you see, know, and experience the true essence of your being, nothing and no one can take that consciousness away from you. You are impervious to human ego or egoistic behavior. When you meditate daily, you move into other dimensions of life. You move beyond the physical plane of existence and discover with time the essence of who you are and the essence of life. With time, as you raise your vibrational frequency, you will be able to see yourself, all beings, and all life as fluid light energy. It is a place of equanimity, perfect peace, boundless bliss, love, and joy. You will discover the source from where everything is possible.

The well-being we experience is a reflection of the internal freedom and love we allow. Freedom is born from within. When the mind is liberated true consciousness is activated and true divine knowledge flows boundlessly.

There is a universal language of the heart by which all life and all beings are connected as one. It is a place of freedom and boundless joy, love, and peace!

YOUR BELIEFS ARE CREATING YOUR PATH

Your beliefs create your reality. You might not be completely aware of all your beliefs. Many are hidden programs embedded within the memory of the cells. Search deep inside the nature of your beliefs and get in touch with your feelings to find your beliefs. Are some of your beliefs associated with chronic fears? Write a list of your beliefs, and complete your list daily or weekly. You will find many new beliefs. You will soon realize that the reality of your daily experience is reflecting these beliefs. Many of your beliefs may limit your experience of happiness, wellness, and harmony. Learn to recognize them and let them go.

Thoughts and feelings are influenced by beliefs. The nature of your beliefs is magnetized energy contributing to the experience you are manifesting in your life.

If some beliefs are not in alignment with harmonic loving energies, change these beliefs so that they serve higher loving purpose for you and for all life. Choose your beliefs, to reflect expanding creative energies, embracing and inviting goodness, wellness, abundance, love, beauty, bliss, and joy—for you, for all beings, and for all life. Choose what feels infinitely loving and expanding.

In furtherance of your spiritual awakening, you have the ability to let go of all your beliefs peacefully and live in the consciousness of your heart—bathing in that magical divine field of peace love light consciousness from which all of life is sourcing. You are then opening a space to experience divine knowledge, divine creativity, and wisdom. If you notice that you still have beliefs, invite them to be in the flow of peace, reverence, love, and light. You are reprogramming the memory of your cells in a very conscious and positive way. Every step toward increasing harmony and love activates a doorway of light where love flows boundlessly.

> *Every moment, I love moving into higher dimensions of my being.*
>
> **I create my path, living in true consciousness, and as I am the observer of my beliefs, I always remember who I am.**
>
> *I am love life force synergy, breathing in the oneness of the sacred light and holy mind of God.*

HOW TO EMPOWER YOUR LIFE WITH JOY

If you wish to attract your most compatible manifesting soul partner, the process is always the same. If you come from a place of despair, emptiness, and pain, you will not attract the person you are truly wishing for. If you don't feel whole and joyous, you will not attract someone who feels whole and joyous. You naturally attract someone with similar vibrations and issues.

If you wish for harmony in your relationships, learn to create within you the energy of wellness and joy. Find in "you" the energy frequency you wish to attract. Dive into the consciousness of your divine Self.

If you are desperate and hopeless to feel loved and to experience love, pay attention to these painful feelings. Dwelling on despair invites energies you don't want. Shake up and start a healing process that is of love and nurturing. Transform the feelings of despair. Learn to love "you" and invite positive visions about you and your life. Learn to embrace the goodness and beauty of your world. Learn to give and receive with love and grace.

Love, faith, well-being, and happiness have to be awakened from deep within you—from God's consciousness of love within you.

Learn to experience in you the loving qualities of the man or woman you would like to attract as your most compatible soul mate. You have the ability to heal and awaken these qualities within you.

Observe with love in your heart a flower, a sunset, a child, or an animal companion. Learn to open the heart. Learn to connect with life from your heart. You will activate a flow of love and joy moving through you boundlessly. Visualize a bright light endlessly expanding from your heart. Stay aware of your breathing and experience the love light all around you and emanating from you. Extend that love light from your heart to all beings and all of life. Slowly come back in your heart and breathe deeply and slowly all the love of the world and the love emanating from your being—as one. Learn to experience your bond with the beauty and sacredness of life.

Express gratitude for all the beauty and love emanating from all life.

Write about the person you would like to bring into your life.

You would like him or her to be kind, honoring, loving, joyous, fun, successful, caring, giving, intelligent, and healthy. Describe him or her on all levels. As you contemplate your words, see if your vibrations match the vibrations of the person you would like to attract in your life. Become aware of the nature of your vibrations. Meditate to align your consciousness with these qualities. Live expressing these qualities. Live within these high frequencies in every moment—as if this person would be with you. Your heart overflows with joy and appreciation.

I lovingly empower my being and life with vibrational frequencies of gratitude, appreciation, and joy radiating from the core essence of my being, my God–Self. I feel a holy protection and flow of love emanating from these blessings.

True Power of Thoughts, Feelings, Emotions, Intentions, Beliefs, and Words

Sporadic conflicts around the globe, misery, and suffering represent wave frequencies born from human egos. They are created from unconsciousness and ignorance of the God-Self.
If you wish for peace and harmony on the planet, find peace in "you". This is how powerful every human being is! We are one!
Thoughts, feelings, emotions, intentions, beliefs, and words emanate energy frequencies. Human beings have the capacity to create warfare or invite peace and harmony. Which level of consciousness do you choose?

Ruling political powers around the world using mind control methods to gain power originate from fear and greed—the ego has control over the personality. It is unconsciousness. It is reflecting people's forgetfulness about their true divine nature and oneness with Source. They have forgotten the way of the heart. The way of the heart is of pure love consciousness. It has the power to bring forth Heaven on Earth. It is a place of inner freedom and peace!

Misery around the world mirrors humankind's inner state of chaos and pain, including people's self-imposed, destructive mental restrictions and indoctrinations. The physical, mental, and emotional planes are cloistered with self-imposed restrictions that are too often derived from bigotry, inequity, control, discrimination, prejudice, greed, and hatred. If you feel that you need to step outside of a matrix of fear, suffering, and illusion, make a conscious decision to meditate, to nurture yourself, and choose love. Now is the time to free your path to know your oneness with all creation and to invite reverence, love, and grace. Remember who you are!

People who have lost an awareness of their divinity are usually gullible, since they are not grounded in true consciousness. They are easily influenced and conditioned by media, negative political views, and beliefs.

It is painful to feel disconnected from God—whether it is a conscious state or not.

When a vast majority of people decide to live within a consciousness of the heart, we shall naturally invite, choose, and manifest governments and leaders working for everyone's highest good—honoring all life's beauty, natural resources, and sacredness. For peace, goodness, and harmony to prevail, we all have to awaken and live within a consciousness of the heart of the soul.

Now is the time for every human being to activate the unified heart and awaken to a consciousness of sacredness and holiness within all of creation. This awakening is activated within our DNA, RNA, and cells—within our bodies and hearts. Doorways of light are opening for all beings to move through, to embrace a consciousness of their divinity and light.

The Tree of Life with all aspects of God is activated within all human beings at this time. Every human being has the ability to connect with his or her true identity and awaken. As more people choose the path of love and awareness, goodness and harmony intensify on the planet.

Denying our spiritual awakening is denying the fundamental aspect of who we are. It is a place of separation, aloneness, and suffering.

It is fundamental to reach the realization that it is possible to live in peace and love one another.

The quintessence of all life is a divine design and frequency of pure love synergy in action, forever evolving, expanding, and transforming. It is an intelligent field of light energy in action and we are one with it.

When you truly understand the energetic power of every word, thought, wish, intention, and belief, you shall choose them to be of love, beauty, compassion, and honoring. Together, they represent an extended frequency of the awareness you are choosing in every moment.
You have the ability to choose your words, thoughts, intentions, and beliefs to be expanded energies of your divine Self. Learn to live with awareness. Learn to live from your beautiful spiritual Self—the qualities of the heart and the soul.

You are a gift to all life. Be the gift of love you are meant to experience!

People who spread and support violence, hatred, and war in the name of freedom and power are unfortunately ignoring their true divine and sacred nature. The way they are looking for freedom will never lead them to freedom. The way they are looking for power will never lead them to true power. They choose a path leading to suffering and chaos. It is a state of ignorance and blindness.

Respond to fear and hatred with forgiveness, compassion, and love. The power of love is infinite. It is only through forgiveness, compassion, and love that you bring someone back to love. You are helping them remembering who they are. Forgiveness and compassion open and activate a consciousness of the heart—it is love consciousness.

During these global changes, it is essential to step out from an illusory matrix—to come together as conscious beings of light, holding sacred space and working together in reverence.

With Mother Earth, we are moving toward higher dimensions of light. It is a consciousness of the heart. We have an opportunity to come together in love and honoring, and live in harmony with the Earth Being, and all nature's intelligence.

The power of love is unlimited. When great numbers of people unite with altruistic intentions and thoughts of peace, joy, compassion, and reverence, it opens doorways of infinite goodness—and love flows. **We are united within one consciousness of the heart, and we have the ability to create a world where every being lives in harmony and peace.**

Compassion and love prevail, once the veil of illusion and ignorance has faded, liberating a sense of true identity and oneness.

Now is the time to remember our sacredness and all sacred aspects of life! Remember!

Imagine a world free of borders, where we trade services, helping, honoring, and loving one another, embracing our oneness—and embracing an evolving, empowering process of bliss, joy, harmony, reverence, and love.

For too many people, the idea of a peaceful, harmonious world is utopist or a fantasy. You can see here how such beliefs limit the ability to bring forth peace and to live in true consciousness. There are worlds where harmony, unconditional love, and peace prevail and flow. As conscious beings, we have the ability and the undeniable potential to create in harmony such peaceful world. All we have to do is allow and embrace love light flow, living from a consciousness of the heart.

Shine your light! Love all life!

Find loving nurturing peace in you, reconcile with all life, and embrace a harmonious relationship with all of life. Joy comes from an open heart and a true consciousness of the Self.

Since Mother Earth is moving toward higher dimensions of the light, the magnetic forces emanating from your beliefs, thoughts, and feelings are increasingly more powerful. They manifest faster within the world of physicality. In every moment, you are creating. Choose to create in love!

Remember that complaining, blaming, or judging—as well as having feelings of anger, condemnation, guilt, bigotry, and resentment—confine you. They restrict you 100 percent in your creative manifesting power toward happiness. Such behaviors hold you in a space that is preventing you from being all of who you are and receiving all you wish for and deserve.

Living within an enlightened consciousness is to emanate blissful serenity. It is living your purpose and loving all beings. Every day, you have the ability to walk on that path.

> *I am honoring the full expression and emanation of my being in love. I choose to live as full energetic consciousness of Source, forever living the gift of grace, blissful harmony, and goodness. I choose to contribute to a world of peace and harmony. I am loved unconditionally.*

CHAPTER FOUR

Knowing Your True Essence

F EEL, THINK, SPEAK, HEAR, SEE, and act with consciousness. Learn to live your life within the frequency and consciousness of your essence, your God-Self, and the quintessence of all life.

HOW TO KNOW MY TRUE ESSENCE

I open my heart, allowing the energetic expression of my sacredness and oneness to be revealed.

As I move into the realization of my spiritual quintessence, I naturally let go of all resistance. All fears are then transmuted into love.

It is in the awareness of my divine presence that grace, divinity, and joy are revealed to me boundlessly. I experience love in boundless ways.

As I choose and learn to walk through life from a consciousness of the heart, my true nature is revealed. In every moment I learn to live in the reality and frequency of my spiritual quintessence.

Everyone is longing for the experience of his or her quintessence that it is lived with consciousness or not. If you wish to live with awareness, you will take steps to progress toward higher consciousness and meditate daily.

The level of intensity of suffering, struggle, and despair one experiences reflects the level of one's attachments to the illusory aspect of the material-physical world. The ego, fed by a multitude of thoughts and illusory beliefs, is then in charge, creating a veil that is hiding truth and true consciousness.

Challenges are on your path to teach you, shape you and lead you to a higher place of consciousness—a place where you shine your light to help all beings. Through deep inner contemplation, meditation, and spiritual work, the personality works with Spirit and from the heart—the ego fades away. It is a divine union and an experience of the soul.

Moving into harmonic alignment with one's true Self is healing. **To me, the word "healing" means, moving back into living within a consciousness of love and of the sacred. It is experiencing that source of infinite love and light that springs from all life and from within you.**

Every time you let go of energies that are not serving you positively, you are actually moving closer to experiencing your quintessence.

Your inner state is an accurate reflection of the world you choose to perceive in the moment. You have free will to transform that perception any time you wish. You have the ability to change your perspective about any situation, capture the wisdom in it, and express compassionate love. You inner state mirrors the level of awareness you are willing to allow.

If you wish to know about your true essence and live within its frequency of love, it is important that you take time to meditate, pray, practice spiritual work, and activate this source of infinite love within your heart. It is also important that you understand and live your life's purpose.

Every morning and every evening meditate for about twenty minutes or more—or meditate when you have a few minutes. In your meditation, gently free your mind from all thoughts and focus on your breath. If you are spending time in nature, focus on the sounds in nature; it will bring you a sense of well-being and serenity.

Some people like to meditate with mantras emanating high-energy frequencies of peace, love, and light. Mantras are guiding you to serenity. They calm the mind and relax your whole being. High frequencies always activate light in your beingness. They have the capacity to clear your field and reprogram the cells with peace love light life force. They activate life energetic flow.

> *I move into new dimensions of my being and of life that are*
> *holy and of boundless love.*

If you feel that you need support and guidance to learn meditation, there are beautiful centers all around the world open to all people from all faiths. For example, *Vipassana Meditation* is an organization with centers all around the world. They teach meditation. It is open to all human beings who wish to experience meditation in a nurturing loving environment.

> *J. Krishnamurti said, "Meditation is the freedom from thought, and a*
> *movement in the ecstasy of truth."*

In order to experience your oneness with all creation and to experience your divinity, learn to step outside a matrix of pain and move into a new reality of loving-kindness that is infinitely nurturing. Learn to be aware of the divine presence of God lovingly holding you in the light.

Choose to be true to "you". Look at your life objectively to see what needs to be harmonized and nurtured.

You cannot change other people's behaviors or decisions, but you can change your perception in any moment.

Commit to practice inner spiritual work, prayers, and meditations. Commit to love.

> *I am living within the consciousness of my essence where bliss, serenity, and joy are experienced from within, allowing my light to shine. It is God expressed in me!*
> *I am whole and free.*

The power of love is everlastingly expressed throughout the whole creation, omnipresent, omnipotent, and forever embedded within you and all of creation.

Living from a place of reverence, love, and honoring benefits all life. Giving and receiving are similar energies; both parties have to open the heart to receive in love and to give in love. Both are gifts!

How to Live in Harmonic Alignment with your True Essence

Witness the power of your faith and love in action. Live in the consciousness of your heart, and you will be naturally guided. Trust, stay aware of your intentions, and choose them of love. Place yourself in God's loving care.

Any moment, you have the ability to allow divine energetic alignment. Choose your intentions to always serve the highest good in all life. You are not walking alone. Pay attention to the divine guidance life is offering in every moment. Witness the miracles in your daily life the moment you choose to move with ease and peace with the flow of live. Sustain an awareness of love's flow and act within that same frequency.

Divine guidance is inherently within you every moment of your existence. God is always with you and within you. The archangels, angels of light, your divine guidance team, and ascended masters are eager to help and guide you within God's love and light.

You are light within the light. You are a ray of light shinning in the radiance of God. Rest in peace in the consciousness of your essence and witness the miracles of life. Live your purpose.

In a difficult and challenging situation, create sacred space by consciously connecting with God's love and light. Call in your master guides, ascended masters, archangels, and angels of the light for help, guidance, strength, and clarity. Create a sacred space that is nurturing to you—within God's light.

Within God's light, call upon the violet flame to be placed in the middle of that situation, embracing everyone and everything involved. Express the intention to hold that space within God's highest consciousness of love and light. Then ask for beautiful pink love light force energy from God to embrace everyone. This pink love light is moving through everyone's heart center too. Open your heart to receive the blessings of love, allow the shift. Then ask for a beautiful rainbow to lovingly embrace everyone.

Place your hands on your heart and give thanks to all life, to the beings of light, and to God. In your heart, anchor the love light of the experience.

God is with me always.

I cannot emphasize enough how many times in my life I have witnessed the power of love and light harmonizing challenging situations in the most unexpected ways. Energetic harmonization is in action the moment you have the ability to open your heart to receive. Move beyond what is and be the observer. Call upon divine assistance, God's love light. You are inviting and allowing the forces of love to be expressed and flow.

Your light body is awakened when your thoughts, intentions, and feelings hold compassion and love, when you have moved into a new paradigm of your being that is sacred and holy, and when you serve all life in love.

> *My whole being and consciousness move into higher dimensions of light. I choose to live within as well as beyond five dimensional frequencies and consciousness. The expression of my divine essence is limitless.*

Every time you free yourself from painful feelings, resentments, and judgments, you are embracing increasing love, happiness, and harmony, and you are moving closer to your true divine nature.

Experiencing your spiritual essence is experiencing oneness and divine bliss.

I would like to share with you an event in my life, illustrating the importance of such awareness—and how to shift the course of an unpleasant situation.

> *A long time ago, I was moving back to the mainland after living several years on a few islands in the Pacific. I was sad to leave behind me such wonderful, harmonious, and blessed times. But I made the decision to move back to the mainland anyway. Obviously, my vibrations were not at the highest. I was staying at my girlfriends' house until I could find my new home. I looked and looked, but I could not make up my mind. I was not taking the time to project, visualize, and ask clearly for what I really needed and wanted. My vibrations were quite low. I felt sad to leave such beautiful times and places. I received a phone call from the moving company about my shipment arriving within a week. I had to find my home in the next two weeks.*

> *Because of this time pressure (I was in reality imposing on myself— something I didn't have to do!), I choose a home I didn't really like. I was confused and was not realizing I was losing my power and the awareness of my free will, choices, and creative potential. My energy was scattered by negative feelings, instead of being positively creative and anchored in the present. I could have created exactly the home I needed—if I had cleared up*

my thoughts and feelings to connect with the serenity of my presence (the way I have done it in the past, in other situations—projecting and visualizing a new home with enthusiasm and joy).

Prior to moving into my new home, the manager assured me that the place was going to be perfectly cleaned. The day I moved in, I found out that it had not been cleaned very well, and the carpet had stains.
This situation aggravated me even more. Without realizing it, I kept lowering my vibrations; therefore, I was still losing my power and moving away from my divine presence and awareness.

I called the owner and manager. We planned to meet a couple of days later. The meeting was a nightmare, and the owner kept screaming and cursing. This really shook me up! When they left, I finally realized I had unconsciously created the whole situation. I had to do something to move out from my negative state of mind, feeling sorry for myself and disempowered. After the meeting, the vibrations in the home were so low that I was suffocating on all levels. I was feeling sick. I could barely breathe. It woke me up!

I decided to take action right away. I started to burn sage while I was praying, clearing up all the spaces around me, including the space between the owner, the manager, and me. At the same time, I was uplifting my vibrations. I was purifying the place, releasing all unbalanced and negative energies into the light of God. I was sending energies of forgiveness, compassion, gratitude, and love to the manager and the owner. I was clearing and cleaning the place with feelings of gratefulness and love, opening my heart. I was coming back home, within myself, and connecting with my God-Self.

A few days later, the manager called me to let me know that the owner decided to give me two months of free rent, and that someone would come over to clean the carpet. I was amazed by that shift of energy and grateful for the experience. I decided to stay in the home for about a year, sustaining high vibrations, nurturing myself with feelings of gratitude and joy to have a safe home, and having the consciousness and ability to create my future in the eternal present. What a great lesson! What a great experience!

This experience taught me to be far more aware of my intentions, feelings, and thoughts—and to be aware of what I choose to create in my life in every moment. I understood, with even further clarity, our ability to create with awareness and gratitude—trusting the process of life. It taught me to always remember the divinity of my beingness and to live within that consciousness.

I learn and grow from my experiences with ease and gratitude. My experiences empower my awareness and willingness to trust and love all life.

The power of love and gratitude uplifted the situation in the most unexpected and surprising ways. Life endlessly teaches us and guides us, moving us toward harmony, goodness, and an awareness of the sacred. All is energy. With time, we learn about the power of love and of the light inherent in all al life.

Toward the end of the first year, I created my new home, visualizing what I wanted with feelings of expectancy and joy. I moved in my new home with infinite gratitude in my heart.

Challenges are blessings when we choose to look for the wisdom they offer. We always have the ability to consciously choose how we respond to life.

At any moment, we are able to choose the nature of our vibrations with consciousness.

If you are looking for changes in your life, choose to move through the changes with love, grace, serenity, and gratefulness in your heart—it is true Power.

You don't need to hate a situation or place in order to create changes. It will only create disharmony, chaos, and pain. You will take these low energies with you and create something you don't want.
If you wish to create something new, create your vision within the serenity and love of your being, trusting the outcome of your energetic

projection. Take baby steps toward your goals; soon the baby steps become big steps. Feel grateful for all that life is giving you in every moment. Praise life and have fun creating in every moment of your life!

Take responsibility and learn with grace the lessons that life is offering you. Count your blessings. Become a source of clarity, love, and harmony. Gain trust, strength, and wisdom. Strength comes from love.

My strength is the strength of God.

If there is any energy within your being that is not in alignment with your divine Self or God-Self, life is going to bring forth a situation that will help you identifying that unbalanced vibration. This will happen until you wake up! It is up to you to see the blessing in it. It is your free will to recognize it, release it, and harmonize it. It is your free will to trust and choose love. It is never too late to choose love.

I choose to be anchored in the consciousness of my heart.
I breathe from that sacred space of boundless love.

ALL OF LIFE IS IN SYNERGY WITH YOUR TRUE ESSENCE

Every time you choose love, you are contributing to global transcendence toward higher dimensions of light—you are contributing to peace and harmony.

Release all resistances. Open a space to embrace awareness and sacredness.

The moment you are free from all doubts, negative thought forms, and patterns, you invite a consciousness of love to manifest harmoniously in all aspects of your life. You are then in harmonic alignment with your beingness, your true essence, and with all life. You are living your purpose, embracing blissful serenity.

No veil of illusion blocks the vision of who you are at the core of your being.

All of "who you are" is energetically, synergistically, and intimately working in harmonic oneness with the sacred laws—the laws of nature. The sacred laws are in action within infinite synergies of vibrational geometrical light patterns, divinely orchestrated. It is a divine design and intelligence—a field of light and energy. You are one with it. Your whole beingness is operating and vibrating with and within the divine geometrics of the sacred laws in perfect synchronicity. Your whole beingness is intrinsically vibrating with and within this intelligent field of light.

Whatever your path and choices in life, you are always subject to the sacred laws of nature. Your vibrational design works in oneness with them. Choosing love, compassion, and honoring is walking harmoniously within the sacred laws. It is your natural state of being— your true essence expressed.

Within the sacred laws of nature, a divine harmonic design encompasses all of life. It is the Flower of Life, encompassing all sacred geometry. This divine design encompasses the Tree of Life, guiding every human being to live the way of the heart. We belong to an intelligent divine matrix sourcing from the heart of all creation. All qualities of God emanate from the Tree of Life and are embedded within the Flower of Life.
All qualities of God are seeded in our spiritual and genetic design.

When the Tree of Life is activated within you, you live in bliss.

All laws in nature are perfectly interconnected, emanating an energetic geometrical-mathematical, light, and sound harmonic synergy. Some of the laws are the law of gravity, the law of time, the law of light, the law of the mind, the law of truth, the law of cause and effect, the law of sound, the law of magnetism, the law of creation, the law of attraction, and the like.

What we do to others, we do to ourselves. It is law. All laws are working in harmonic synergy.

The quintessence of all life consists of an intelligent field of love light energy synergy working in perfect divine harmony.

The sacred laws cannot be avoided or changed. All sacred laws are working as one matrix encompassing all of creation.
Our molecular vibrational structure and magnetic field frequency on all levels are in perfect oneness and symbiosis with the magnetic "mind" matrix, holding all sacred laws, encompassing all aspects of God, our point of essence, and the Tree of Life. **We are living within the oneness of an intelligent divine design.**

All beings and all of life are synergistically divinely operated and coded in oneness within a worldwide, cosmic, intelligent, and magnetic field of light—a matrix of love light from which all forms spring. This intelligent magnetic field of light or grid is embedded within the core of all beings and all of life. It is a divine design that belongs to God.

A newly programmed intelligent magnetic field of light is facilitating our awakening toward higher dimensions of the light—reprogramming our cells, DNA/RNA, and activating our light bodies!

This field of light is holding infinite rays of light, divinely programmed throughout all of creation. They are also anchored within Mother Earth, serving divine purposes—in service to Mother Nature, encompassing all nature's intelligence with the animal kingdom.

Such a divine, geometrical matrix of light lives embedded within all forms of life and creation, and within us. This is why we are living and breathing with the Earth Being and all life. Whatever we do, express, and choose has a ripple energetic effect touching all beings and life.

Now is the time for all human beings to awaken to a consciousness of oneness and unity consciousness. Now is the time to understand and revere the wonders and holiness of life!

YOU ARE LIGHT

Freedom is in the light. Light is of pure love frequency. Light is the source of all that is. You are of light frequency. You are light.

Mother Theresa was a true living example. She revealed the true power of the light in all aspects of her life. She was unconditionally loving and compassionate toward all beings—forever free of all judgment. The light emanating from her beingness holds a sempiternal magnetic field of God's grace, peace, and unconditional love, uplifting and permeating all life in holiness—to this day.

Today, numerous light workers and emissaries of peace, known and unknown, are emanating the same vibrational persona of light uplifting all beings and opening people's hearts.

> *It feels wonderful to make peace with life. It feels wonderful to make peace with all beings. It feels wonderful to make peace with "me". Life is lovingly supporting me. It feels wonderful to be loved by all life. All life is nurturing me, loving me. I bathe in the One Source of love and light.*

When you recognize your true nature, knowing and living within true consciousness of your light, you lose all notion of pain. Nothing or no one can change this reality or take it away. This is when all false illusory identification born from the ego, dissipates. In true consciousness, the ego loses all power and dissolves. You are then a radiant light!

Your social status, your gender, and nationality are not who you are. You are a divine being of light and of God. Whether you are rich or poor, from Australia or Africa, from America, Europe, or Asia, reaching true consciousness has nothing to do with your nationality or your social-economic status. You are from a source of love and light consciousness.

Your Heart is a radiant sun illuminating your mind. You then experience your sacredness—the consciousness of God within you and emanating from all life.

I open the Stargate of my heart, honoring the supreme light, in the full realization of my essence.

LIVING IN AWARENESS OF YOUR TRUE ESSENCE

It is important to acknowledge all your feelings so that you can learn to be aware of the energetic frequency you emanate—and learn to live with consciousness. You have then the ability to make choices from a place of clarity and let go of what does not serve higher purposes.

Your divine presence, God-Self, or divine Self has nothing to do with thought forms, beliefs, possessions, or anything you have done or accomplished. Your God-Self is of peace love light consciousness. You are a divine design of light. Use your God-given gifts to bring forth goodness, joy, and beauty in your world.

If you learn to understand and recognize the ego when it shows up, it is easy to sustain an awareness of your true identity and live within that consciousness.
Holding on to chronic fears and illusory beliefs blinds you. The ego likes to distort reality. Chronic fears are encouraged by the ego.

It is easy to recognize your divine guidance team and God's messages. It is a vibration and emanation of peace, love, light, and wisdom—forever living within you. Learn to recognize that emanation within the stillness of your heart.

Learn to identify the nature of your feelings and emotions within the awareness of the heart.

If you are scattered and confused, please do not panic. Take a lot of time to calm your mind and emotions so that you are able to listen to your heart. Pray and meditate. Focus on the breath. Breathe peace love light in all your being and heart. Release into the light of God all confusion and pain. When you are calm and more connected within your inner being and heart, observe gently all thoughts passing by. Allow them to pass by and fade away with ease. Do not give any more power to these thoughts. Let them pass by with ease. Focus on your breathing until all thoughts are gone and until you dance in the nurturing love of your breathing. Continue this meditation until you experience blissful peace—and you will know who you are.

Divine guidance comes about naturally when you open the space of your heart, and when you free the mind.

There is infinite divine guidance and assistance available to every human being. Your prayers and heart's desires are always answered in ways that are serving your spiritual growth and highest best, guiding you to a consciousness of the heart of your soul—your divine essence. Life is always leading you to true divine consciousness, since it is life's true essence.

When you are at peace, living within the consciousness of your essence, it does not mean that you have lost your feelings. Your beautiful feelings and emotions are still with you, guiding you in your life, but your awareness with your inner foundation of blissful serenity is making all the difference. You will not feel overwhelmed by your emotions and feelings anymore. The difference is that you know how to recognize the ego. You have learned to live with your thoughts and feelings in ways that will not affect your inner peace, awareness, and joy. You know how to transform them in loving and nurturing energies. You know who you are.

Move through life in the oneness of the heart guided by divine wisdom. Insecurity and despair no longer control your existence.

Awaken your consciousness to the sempiternity presence of the light.

When the mind is free from thoughts about the past and the future, you naturally experience the present, breathing in the now—you are conscious of your divine presence. Life becomes a joyous experience.

Ancient Prophecies, sacred texts, indigenous cultures, and elders speak of a new age, a golden age, where we are all awakened. Every human being has the opportunity to move harmoniously with the flow of this awakening.

Our bodies of light are awakening and the physical body is transmuting at the core of its cellular structure. Since we are moving toward higher dimensions of light our physical cellular structure is naturally transforming into higher frequencies of light energy. In other words, our physical body is slowly and progressively fusing energetically with our light body. We will see to what degree this transmutation occurs with the passage of time. This transmutation is based upon achieving a life of pure love consciousness—living from the God-Self. It is a process activated by an awakening and illumination of the unified heart—the heart of the soul—and an illumination of the mind. The light of our whole beingness—encompassing the energetic emanation of the physical body—becomes further perceivable and visible as one radiant light.

Let go of all resistance and open your heart to experience love consciousness. The heart with the pituitary gland and pineal gland (third eye) keep emanating at their core the same divine holy energies, vibrating by their nature within high dimensions and frequencies of peace love light. Allowing the activation of these divine centers is choosing a consciousness of love, reverence, and unity—it is inviting God's holy rays to infuse them with light.

The moment the pineal gland and the pituitary gland vibrate in synchronicity, they liberate light consciousness—there is an illumination of the God-Self. Sacred light flows and is activated through all energy centers and through all bodies—all the way to the cells and DNA/ RNA.

The pineal gland, also called the pineal body or epiphysis, is a small endocrine gland in the brain. It is located in the center of the brain, behind and just above the pituitary gland, which is called the seat of

133

illumination, intuition, and cosmic consciousness. They work together, connected to our intuition and reason, activating light consciousness from the love emanating from the heart.

Since our cellular structure is transmuted and uplifted to a lighter energetic design, people are awakened, choosing a consciousness of the heart—although, every human being has the choice to embrace that flow or not.
It is a painful place to deny your true nature and not welcome the natural evolution and awakening of your beautiful spiritual Self.

Throughout this global ascension, children are spiritually awakened and free from karmic issues. Their minds are free, and their hearts are open to love unconditionally. They express their God-given gifts and multidimensionality with ease, the moment we offer them the opportunity and loving support to do so. If they lose their way, it is a cry for love—they are looking to be heard in the midst of the mental chaos surrounding them.

> *I live and breathe within the space of my true identity now.*

> *I experience grace.*

This new era is revealing advanced healing techniques and vibrational technologies to support this transition. They are available to all beings. A considerable number of light beings are uniting to divinely assist all life on all levels during this ascension, contributing to the birth of this new era in the most holy ways. Thank you for being one of these light beings.

THE TREE OF LIFE • A PORTAL TO YOUR GOD-SELF

The Tree of Life, within every being and embedded within all life, is activated as we enter higher dimensions and consciousness of light. Our divine design is activated.

The Tree of Life encompasses all twelve aspects God. They represent our fundamental divine qualities embedded within the core essence of our being. They represent twelve doorways of light.

(I am inviting you to view the artwork I have created in my book entitled Twelve Doorways of Light: Sacredness of Life. This artwork is also available on my website: artfromthelight.com)

Through spiritual work, meditation, and love consciousness, we awaken to these aspects of God and live them from the heart. Every time we surrender and embrace the realization of one aspect of God, we are guided through a doorway of light, which moves us closer to the realization of our God-Self.

When the heart opens, recognizes, and embraces all aspects of God or qualities of God, we are led through twelve doorways of light. Walking through these twelve doorways of light and living within their energetic frequencies, invites with unconditional love the emanation of the divine feminine (aspect of God), activating the portal to our God-Self. This divine portal of light invites Heaven on Earth—unity consciousness and peace on Earth.

We experience the heart and mind of God, unity consciousness, and our multidimensionality. The Tree of Life is revealed in its wholeness (read additional insights about the Tree in chapter six). This book is leading you to this experience—it is an experience of your God-Self.

Prayer and meditation:
As I open my heart, I lovingly embrace the divine masculine and the divine feminine with all qualities of God. I am led through twelve doorways of light. Living within the vibrational frequencies of these doorways of light, invites with unconditional love the ultimate emanation of the divine feminine, activating the portal to my God-Self. This divine portal is leading my whole beingness into higher dimensions of light (the fifth dimension and beyond). From my illuminated heart, a golden white ray expands in love all the way to the heart of Mother Earth and the heart of Father Sky, i.e., the Heavens. I am a ray of light in the radiance of God. I experience divine alignment.

There is now a radiant light of unconditional love emanating from all creation embracing me so gently.
I experience unity consciousness, unconditional love, and the multidimensionality of my true being. The sacred light and love I am breathing in my heart and space is anchoring this reality in my consciousness and beingness forever. I am whole and safe in the heart of God. Boundless peace, love, and gratitude flow from my heart. I live the consciousness of God. I live from my God-Self.

As our consciousness embrace all qualities of God's love, the Tree of Life is activated, liberating high dimensions of light sourcing from the heart of our soul. Dance with grace, harmony, and joy within these new energies.
The Tree of Life is a divine design revealing true divine knowledge—sacredness of the soul and sacredness in all that is.

Every moment, you are learning to walk in God's consciousness, crossing the threshold of a new space reality and stepping beyond the veil of illusion. Your whole being is increasingly vibrating at a higher frequency, bringing forth the expression and expansion of your light body, revealing boundless potentialities in love.
When your intentions are pure, your whole being becomes increasingly brighter and lighter. Your brightness and lightness are embraced by all life in love.

I am inviting you to experience the portal and realm of your God-Self.

CHAPTER FIVE

Connective Awareness with Nature's Divine Energies

THIS AMAZING MAGICAL WORLD WE **live in and wish to experience is initially within us and is subsequently manifesting all around us. We just need to recognize it and walk in divine harmony within its sacred laws through a consciousness of the heart.**

LIVING IN HARMONY

Life is endlessly giving us incredible gifts, but we are often not even aware of these gifts. Now is the time to see these gifts.

God's cosmic and sacred laws are one within an intelligent, energetic matrix of light by which everything is, from which everything comes into form, by which everything is operated, generated, and provided by and for all life. It is a divine science.

Divine science is of love consciousness—of God's consciousness. It is the realm of light, of physics, and of sacred geometrics within the laws, through which all creation is operated—from one consciousness of the supreme divine heart within the Tree of Life and the Flower of Life—the one heart and mind of God.

Within the law, humankind has some aspects of free will and choice. This free will is a gift from life and a path, inviting every individual to live from true consciousness.

There is boundless abundance on the planet for every living being to live in harmony with all life. Unfortunately, great inequality prevails in multiple places around the world and in many aspects of life—pain and misery created by humankind. It is an occurrence created by all human beings who have lost an awareness of their divine nature, their oneness with Mother Earth, all beings, and God. This is about to change—every human being is divinely guided in a challenge to awaken now. This challenge is forever blissful when we surrender and choose grace.

Being caught in illusory feelings and beliefs, such as on going despair, fear, bigotry, and greed, is an experience established on misleading priorities.
For instance, there are people and organizations that are amassing great wealth at the cost of harming other people, animals, and the environment. These occurrences demonstrate unconsciousness, fear, and greed. It is denying the existence of one's God-Self and the divine essence in all that is—however we are at a time of change and awakening.
Happiness and harmony never come from destructive invasive intentions or actions. Happiness and harmony come from love and reverence. It is a consciousness revealing qualities of the heart. It is an awareness of the sacred.

If your priorities are not founded on righteousness, reverence, goodness, compassion, and love for all beings—and if feelings of reverence and love are not naturally associated with everything you do—you are missing the most important aspect of "you" and of your life.
You are missing being aligned with the sacredness and essence of life and of who you truly are. You are then separating from the consciousness of your God-Self. Denying your true identity is a painful place to be.

Everything you do from a place of peace, love, reverence, and joy has a ripple effect, generating goodness, wellness, and global harmony.

Think about money as a tool of peace love light energy to create goodness, wellness, joy, and beauty in your life, in the life of others, and for all beings! Choose to live your purpose to bring joy and well-being.

By loving life, you contribute to a better world. Life mirrors and manifests what you are experiencing within you—whether you are conscious of it or not.

Meditating in nature is an amazing way to calm the mind and move into the sacred, secret consciousness of life. If you have the opportunity to be in nature, focus on the sounds in nature. Breathe with nature—breathe with the Earth Being. The sounds in nature are divine energetic emanations of love. Many people have forgotten the holiness of these vibrational frequencies. Our whole energetic being breathes and lives in divine synergy with the voice and breath of nature.

For example, birds' magical, musical sounds create beautiful, harmonic fields of light and joy all around the planet and vibrate with your field of light. This joy and light energy is moving through the vibrational frequency of your being, fusing with your divine design and all life.

Living in consciousness of nature's divine energies is living in divine consciousness.
It is healing, harmonizing, and activating light consciousness.

> *I have the ability and gift to live within high dimensions of light right now.*
> *I choose to honor all beings, nature's divine intelligence, and the Earth Being.*

SARAH JEANE

OUR ONENESS WITH MOTHER EARTH
AND WITH ALL OF CREATION

It is fundamental to understand our intimate relationship with Mother Earth, the Earth Being, and our sacred connection with nature's intelligence.

Ignoring our oneness with Mother Earth, nature's intelligence, and all of creation, is a form of unconsciousness, often leading to destructive behaviors, destabilizing all life.
When Mother Earth's life force, gifts, and natural resources are misused, her breath is then partially taken away. Since we are so intimately connected with the Earth Being and its resources and all of nature, numerous beings are depleted of life force (breath) in all sorts of ways. On a spiritual and emotional level, people are experiencing aloneness, despair, depression, and insecurity—often leading to greed, hatred, or bigotry. In the physical-material world, it is engendering poverty, starvation, numerous conflicts, and warfare. This is leading to all kind of mental disorders and physical illness. What occurs in our environment and lives mirrors our choices of consciousness.

Every living being has the natural ability and gift to live harmoniously in oneness with Mother Earth and all nature's intelligence—since all of creation synergistically exists within the same matrix of consciousness or same intelligent divine design. Within that divine design, every human has some aspect of free will.

> I now choose to live with awareness my divine union with the Earth Being, honoring and loving all beings and all that is.

Global harmony, peace, health, wealth, goodness, and wellness for all beings, requires that the resources of the planet are used with infinite wisdom, reverence, and praise—with a consciousness of the sacred—always serving all life's highest good. This is possible when

we awaken to our true divinity. It is living in divine consciousness and unity consciousness.

Nothing belongs to us but everything lives and breathes with us. We are living in oneness with all that is. All belongs to God.

Mother Earth embraces all her children. We are all enriched by Mother Earth boundless abundance, beauty, and gifts.
Now is the time to awaken to experience and appreciate these divine qualities and gifts.

When trees and forests are destroyed, when the Earth is polluted with its rivers and oceans, all living beings are hurting, including the Earth Being.
Destroying our natural environment and its biological harmony has detrimental consequences for all beings, Mother Earth, and all aspects of life. The core essence of our "beingness and of all that is" is forever untouched and pure love light consciousness; this is why it is never too late to choose to live in true consciousness.

Mother Nature emanates high frequencies that are divine and intimately connected to our energy field, bodies, minds, and hearts. We receive life force from nature's elements—we continually exchange energies with nature. Fruits, vegetables, plants, trees, air, sun, and water—all nature sustains us—and everything in nature is a sustainable design.

Life force energies are also experienced as vortexes, diverse specific energetic currents emerging from the Earth Being and the cosmos—energies and sounds emanating from all creation, crop circles, crystals, gemstones, rocks, water, fire, flowers, plants, trees, and so much more.

Our whole world holds infinite sacred forces, vibrations, sounds, colors, and lights. They are all fundamental to humans, animals, birds, insects, trees, plants, flowers, water and all that is. We all live in harmonic synergy within an amazing divine design. In order to sustain and experience harmony, we have to live within a consciousness of our oneness and sacredness—and the sacredness within all that is.

Connecting with the sacred and magical aspects of life is experiencing the voices of nature, the whisper of God's love in your heart, and the breath of life. When you live consciously in oneness, nothing of a lower energy created by human thought forms is able to take you away from that bliss. Nothing of a lower energy can enter your space.

Nature offers infinite tools and doorways to awaken and to sustain serenity, bliss, joy, and wellness. Nature offers infinite synergies of light, beauty, and gifts of love.

Meditation, Gi-Gong, Yoga, Tai Shi, and similar spiritual activities are intended to sustain well-being and health. They represent wonderful energetic support, activating your life force from the core of your being.

Energy work, spiritual work, and spiritual activities are guiding you to commune with the energies and forces of life.
Interacting with consciousness with the forces in nature brings you balance and well-being. It increases your life force and your awareness about the sacredness in all life. Activities in nature such as swimming, hiking, bicycling, or horseback riding support your bond with nature.

In nature, contemplate the beauty and bask in that light energy. Fill your heart with joy, hug trees, smell the flowers, and experience the loving presence of all the animals, insects, and birds. Meditate, contemplate, and commune from your heart. Breathe with consciousness! You will receive the experience of another reality of life and of yourself. This reality is anchored in oneness, serenity, joy, love, and harmony.

Most people with great anxiety or serious illness have shallow breathing patterns—their life force is low. When you choose to be conscious of your breathing, you are inviting in your being, in your cells a life force that is sourcing from all life and from within you. "Breathing" is a force uniting you with all life. Being aware of your breathing and deepening your breathing increase your life force, well-being, balance, and health. All of life breathes with you.

Learn to commune with the heart of the Earth Being. Learn to breathe with Mother Earth. She is nurturing you. She guides you to experience your oneness.

Awaken to your fundamental oneness and sacredness with all forces in nature.

Rest next to a tree and connect with it. Send to the tree messages of reverence and love. Experience its love frequency and life force. It balances the energies in your whole being and recharges you. It grounds you into the Earth Being and guides you to connect with the sky or the heavens. Listen to its whisper with reverence. The voices in nature fill your heart with nurturing love and joy.

While lying in the grass, listen to the wind, the birds, and the crickets. They are comforting you and connecting you with the sacred forces and voices in nature and with your Self. Swimming in the ocean cleanses your aura, balances and harmonizes your whole being, and recharges you with life force energies. This magical world of beauty and goodness is infinite. Discover the beauty of your world from a place of reverence and praise.

Learn to listen to nature's intelligence.

Contemplate your life peacefully and pay attention to all that is contributing to the awakening of feelings of love, serenity, and joy. Fill your heart with love and gratitude, breathing deeply and slowly.
When your heart is filled with love and gratitude, move your consciousness slowly above your head. Send all that love far into the sky (the Heavens), all around the Earth and throughout the Universe, and be still. The Universe responds to you, showering you with love light energy. It is a radiant light clearing your space and loving you—it is the love and light of God emanating from all creation. If you see different light colors allow them to move through you naturally. This radiant light is embracing you and is entering through the top of your head, moving through your whole body to the bottom of your feet, and entering the Earth Being. Feel this union of love with the Earth Being—all the way to the heart of the Earth Being.

Now place your forehead on the ground (your forehead is touching the ground). From your heart, send love through your third eye into the Earth Being. Experience your oneness with the Earth Being as a sacred bond of infinite nurturing love. Behold and feel your divine communion of love with the Earth Being. Say, "I commune with love from my heart with the heart of Mother Earth". Boundless love flows between Mother Earth and you. Send love and appreciation to Mother Earth. Pay attention to her response and gifts.

When you are ready, come back up slowly, sitting on your knees or directly on the floor or ground, and express gratitude from your heart.

This love light is filling every cell and atom of your being. Your whole energy field is bathing in light, nurturing you. Repeat this process three or seven times and enjoy your sacred nurturing communion with Mother Earth and the blessings from the Heavens.

The essence of life is of love light energy!

SECRET AND SACREDNESS OF LIFE

Throughout your meditations and prayers, take quality time to experience your sacred communion with Mother Nature—from your heart. Connecting with nature in holy ways brings forth the discovery of your sacred world and its boundless multidimensionality.

In the first chapter, I mentioned radiant white spheres of light energy that are seen in many sacred places around the world. These white glowing spheres are vehicles of light governed by angelic beings and masters of light. These sacred lights and divine vortices are brought into the planetary realm to help the Earth Being and its inhabitants. They harmonize and balance energies on all levels of life, assisting all beings toward higher consciousness of light. They emanate the most radiant love light force frequencies.

These masters of light are assisting us in multidimensional ways, contributing to restoring and sustaining balance within all planes of existence and uplifting all life. They are assisting us in our awakening so we can experience our natural synergy with the highest realms of consciousness and oneness with Source—with God.

It is wonderful to meditate and pray in the presence of these magnificent spheres of light or light beings. If you ask for emotional or physical healing, if you would like to help someone and the world, or are looking for answers and guidance, it is a perfect time to open your heart to receive answers, healing, and blessings of love.

These radiant lights are seen throughout the formation and presence of crop circles, for healing, activation and for harmonizing purposes, embracing with love Mother Earth, all beings, and nature's intelligence.

These radiant lights or divine angelic beings of light and masters of light are present during deep energy healing and clearing sessions. These holy presences are assisting with healing, harmonizing, and clearing work. We are never alone. Divine presences are messengers of God, working with us and assisting us. We have the ability to invite them and work with them.

As we allow love light flow and choose to be of service, we are a conduit for peace and harmony. In the presence of these lights, I have always experienced pure, unconditional love, and blissful serenity, divine protection, and guidance. I have witnessed amazing healings and shifts of consciousness on my clients. It feels as though we are in a vehicle of light—infinitely nurturing and loving. Everything is possible within a space of pure love consciousness—miracles are possible; the heart is open and free.

We have the ability to call upon God's peace love light, divine light beings, ascended masters, our divine guides and master guides, angels of light and archangels when we wish to bless a place, for any healing work, during our daily work, when we create, when we pray, when we express gratitude, and any time we wish to connect on a deeper level. We can choose to live within a sacred space of love and reverence at all times. We invite miracles when we choose to live within a sacred space and consciousness.

While walking and meditating in nature, breathe the light life force energy animating all life. Sit down at the base of a tree or lie down in the middle of a meadow. Take several long and deep breaths until you feel relaxed, let go of your worries and thoughts. Allow your thoughts to pass by. Slowly free your mind. Close your eyes and listen to the sounds. They are soothing and comforting. You now feel so safe and so loved. Listen to the voices in nature.

Commune with the energies of the trees, the flowers, the birds, the sky, the wind, the sun, and all life. They are nurturing you and loving you. Breathe in this infinite nurturing love. You will feel joy, blissful, whole, and ecstatic.

Now, slowly and gently open your eyes and look into the sky. Very gently, direct your attention toward your third eye (located in the center of your forehead) and keep contemplating the sky. You will see multitudes of white little bright lights dancing in the sky and around you.
If you are not successful at first, repeat the exercise. Do not force it. Relax and breathe the love life force. With time, you will witness the light life force energy all around you.
Now direct your attention on the tree not far away from you. Gaze at the tree, as if you would see through the tree, to discover its beautiful aura and energy of light force emanating. All is consciousness. The light energy emanates from the grass and the flowers. It is all around you and in you. It is a life force.
Discover your sacred world with love.

A tree is a living sacred being. It is a sentient living life force. Multitudes of divine life forms exist within its beingness.

Learn to commune with the trees, flowers, grass, rocks, insects, birds, wind, and with all life. Hear their whispers and messages. It is for you to learn, see, and hear on a much deeper level. Learn to commune with the sacredness of life. All is sacred and has to be honored. Praise the trees, flowers, insects, and all that is in your life. They need your love, and you need their love too. We are one consciousness and synergy of love in the heart of God.

The magic of our world is infinite. As I mentioned earlier, the language and sounds of the birds come from high dimensions of light. Their sounds bring forth an energetic field made of high celestial frequencies, expanding all around the globe. You have the ability to commune with these celestial sounds and be uplifted to higher realms of consciousness.

Proceed with the following exercise on a day you feel serene and joyful. It is very important that you feel good. Always learn to emanate serenity and love.

Take the time to find peace within you. Calm your mind. Breathe deeply and slowly. Create sacred space by calling upon the Creator's heart and mind consciousness and light, the archangels and your divine guides of the light. In your sacred space, invite anything that feels wonderful and nurturing, such as flowers, birds, crystals, and dolphins playing in the ocean. Have some fun and just feel good. Meditate until you feel serenity, love, and appreciation in your heart.

When you feel blissful, sit comfortably in front of a large mirror so that you can see your whole body. If you are flexible, sit in the lotus position. Otherwise sit in a chair with a pillow supporting your back so that your back is as straight as possible. It is important to feel comfortable. Close your eyes and breathe deeply and slowly—focus on your breathing. Call upon the light and ask to be embraced by God's peace love light. See yourself in a beam of divine light reaching toward the sky and entering the Earth Being. Breathe love light in your space, your body, and in your heart.

If you still have thoughts, slowly empty your mind—allow the thoughts to fade away. Focus on your breathing. When you feel very relaxed in your breathing, move your consciousness to the center of your forehead or third eye. Open your eyes gently directing your attention toward the center of your forehead in the mirror—your mind is calm and you are aware of your divine presence. Keep breathing very slowly and deeply, sustaining a state of peace and relaxation. Experience your breathing as a nurturing flow of love energy moving through you and nurturing you. Now, every time you inhale slowly, hold your breath as long as you can and then slowly exhale. Inhale deeply, from your stomach all the way to your upper chest—hold your breath (without forcing) and slowly exhale. Keep gazing into the mirror, at your third eye in the middle of your forehead. It must feel comfortable. Do not force anything.

Continue gazing into the mirror. Your attention is directed in the middle of your forehead. Become aware of your whole being in the mirror. Slowly discover the nature of your physical body—you see energy in motion. As you continue with the same breathing pattern you will see the glow of your etheric body and of your whole auric field. Physical matter reveals its true energetic nature.
In the mirror, you will see your physical body losing density and gradually becoming more transparent. Your face in the mirror is changing. You might see other faces. If you see different faces, you may ask who they may be. Feel good and relaxed. Continue with the same manner of breathing until you can see your whole auric field. You are aware of your light and energetic substance. The physical body has faded away and is blending with your whole auric field of light. All is light energy in motion. You might see colors. You see the glow of your aura encompassing the energy of your physical body. You have the ability to witness the life force and light force energy of your beingness and divine presence.
Enjoy the peace, the bliss, and the vision.

When you decide to come back, slow down your deep breathing. Gently close your eyes for a few minutes. Breathe calmly and rest. Feel your physical body. Breathe gently—through your whole body all the way to your feet and under your feet. Open your eyes only when you are ready. Then move very slowly and relax for a while.

In this experience, you discover and understand that the physical body is energy consciousness, a divine life force, sustained by your auric field and soul. Your whole beingness is light energy and divine consciousness.

When your intentions are pure, your whole being becomes brighter and lighter. This brightness and lightness are expressed through all aspects of your being. It is in energetic alignment with the love sourcing from all creation. Your true nature is revealed.

I am light within the light. The qualities and nature of the light are sempiternal, divine, and of unconditional love energy frequency.

All Is Consciousness

Upon our magnificent planet there are countless forms of lives and realms, such as nature's spirits, assisting Mother Earth and assisting us, too—they belong to nature's intelligence or nature's consciousness.

We live in oneness with the realms of the animals, devas, plants, crystals, faeries, and many additional realms. Many beings, and thus consciousness, are watching over the natural balance within the ecosystem: the life and growing of the flowers, trees, fruits, vegetables, the seasons, and multiple aspects of life. They assist the animal kingdom, too. They watch over the process and progress of the entire ecosystem—in harmonic synergy with the cosmic sacred laws. "All that is" lives in oneness within a divine design and grid of light.

Everything has consciousness and holds a form of deva or devas attributed to a specific purpose. For example you have the mountain deva and devas or the water deva and devas. Even your car, your computer, your chair has its individual deva. Your dog has a deva. Remember that since everything is energy consciousness, you constantly communicate with everything through energy frequencies—consciously or unconsciously. Learn to commune with all of life with love and reverence. Devas wish to help and love working with us.

If we do not experience life as nurturing, it is because we live outside of ourselves, and the personality is controlled by the ego. Any moment we can choose to live from the heart and bond with the sacredness of life. The personality is then working in harmony with the soul.

All life is divinely and perfectly orchestrated. Life is loving and caring for itself and infinitely nurturing. Bask in that energy consciousness and remember the sacredness. Peacefully commune with love with your surrounding.

> *I commune with all forms and expressions of life with reverence.*
> *I commune with all creation from my heart.*
> *I praise all life in gratitude and remember who I am.*

It is essential for humankind to revere and praise the divine synergies in nature, a network of intelligence and light within the ecosystem. When we respect nature's spirits and nature's laws, we respect ourselves and immensely enhance our lives and our well-being.

For example, if you wish to remove weeds in your yard, do not use herbicides. These poisons used commercially are very harmful to you and the environment. They are sold freely, and most gardeners are using them without knowing the tremendous damage they are causing to the ecosystem, the water, insects, animals, pets, and children, and themselves.

Most of these dangerous herbicides and pesticides have already been banned in a few countries because of their harmful components. Additionally, underground water sources are being contaminated, killing insects and animals, and seriously damaging the ecosystem. Please be aware of what you spray—and where your children and animals play. Revere the Earth Being with all its inhabitants.

The ecosystem is an intelligent design and synergy in action encompassing the Earth Being, all beings, and nature's intelligence. Within its divine design, it sustains and encompasses all levels and purpose of life.

When humans disrespect and destroy the harmonic synergies and interaction of life within the ecosystem, all life is affected and is hurt. There are always natural and gentle ways to attend to your garden and home. Educate yourself and look for these natural ways. Learn to communicate with nature in reverence and love—remember always that all is consciousness and that all is one.

Today millions of bees are dead or dying. If we kill bees and insects, we hurt all life. Bees are pollinators. Bees give us much more than honey. They enable plants to produce the fruits we eat, by carrying pollen from one plant or flower to the next.
Using pesticides and herbicides is destroying our food supplies. It is harming all beings and Mother Earth. It gives power to the production of genetically-modified foods, causing great harm to all beings and all of life. Now is the time for every human being to make conscious choices.

I love the bees and butterflies and respect all the insects in my garden. I choose to keep my home clean so that they almost never come into my home to look for food or shelter. I am honoring their space and I ask them to honor my space. We live in harmony.

Honoring life is honoring "you"!

Living in sacred ways is recognizing your oneness with all beings, nature, the Earth, and all creation, breathing love consciousness.

Trees, flowers, rocks, the wind, the sun, the rain, the planets, and the animals—everything in your world has consciousness.
As you meditate in nature and connect with nature's intelligence with praise and from the heart, it is a wonderful way to connect with your true Self and make peace with all life. I wish you a magical time, basking in the light and beauty of nature.

Deepen your love for Mother Earth and all its inhabitants.

NATURE'S INTELLIGENCE

Every form and expression of life has a deva or devas—even technological and scientific inventions. Devas belong to nature's consciousness. The devic realm is associated with the realm of nature's spirits, all nature's intelligence, including fairies, gnomes, and water and garden's spirits.

Since devas belong to nature's intelligence, specific missions are embedded and coded within their divine design in harmonic synergy with nature's sacred laws. Devas sustain nature's harmony within the ecosystem and all of life, in accordance with sacred laws.

Devas are generally focused on one specific mission. For example the deva of a flower is interested in the growth, beauty, and well-being of that flower. The deva of my dog companion is interested in sustaining his well-being.
Devas enjoy to be of assistance. They wish to help in beneficial ways. We have the ability to communicate and work with devas to receive their nurturing loving assistance—to serve all life in beautiful ways. Devas live in harmonic synergy and oneness with all of life.

Angels have specific missions and purposes, assisting us and assisting all of life in countless ways.

Learning to communicate with nature's intelligence or nature's spirits on deep and conscious levels increases awareness and expands your love for the sacredness of life. It is an aspect of life that you discover gradually when you choose to make peace with life—and truly connect from deep levels of your being with life.

As your awareness and love for life expands, you realize the Earth is a living, breathing being with consciousness.
Communicating with nature's intelligence changes your life in the most surprising ways. It helps you to develop the ability to emanate deeper qualities of honoring and divine connectivity in all circumstances. It opens your heart.

Since many people have lost consciousness of these divine intelligent forces in nature, much damage has been done within that realm. Through these words, I choose to be a voice of awareness for all human beings about this issue so that we all wake up and learn to live in infinite honoring, revering all life and Mother Earth.

The devic realm is working diligently to clear up damage, chaos, and pollution. There are people on the planet who have developed a close connection with the devic realm. Together, they are healing the Earth Being. They are helping our environment, clearing up pollution and working on sustaining balance. You have the ability to do the same. I invite you to join me on that path. You will love the journey!

Love the Earth Being!

Our Sacred Connection with the Animal Kingdom and Nature's Intelligence

The love I feel for animals—and from animals—has such an important place in my heart and in my life.
I have been inspired to share personal insights and experiences related to the animal kingdom—how to understand animals and communicate with them from a place of love.
I am sure you have amazing stories to share. Please share your stories— they raise awareness and bring forth joy, love, and healing.

Within the animal realm, we find diverse characteristics of evolution. All species of life have to be held in high regard. All species have to be recognized as sacred and respected. All species have an intrinsic birthright to live in harmonic synergy within the ecosystem.
Animals are participating in our global ascension. They participate in a different way than we humans do.

Animals respond to life according to their specific extrasensory abilities, their purpose, and their realm, Mother Nature, and the energies they receive from their environment. They recognize energies without distortion because they don't have any ego. That is why animals always tell the truth. They communicate from and through energies.

Since they are free from the ego, they are naturally in touch with multidimensional aspects of consciousness. Their spirits are free. If people around them live from a consciousness of the heart, they naturally live and evolve in harmony with their environment. Animals are breathing with the Earth Being and live in harmonic synergy with Mother Nature, their realm of consciousness.

I believe that animals have special gifts. They have an instinctive intelligence that is pure. They know about love energies and they recognize fear energies. Since they perceive everything through vibration frequencies, they recognize energies without distortion.

Animals are in our lives for various reasons. They know how to open our hearts and teach us unconditional love. They come into our lives for specific purposes and missions. Their paths are different than ours because they live their purpose differently than we do. We have so much to learn from them.
Their extrasensory, telepathic, and intuitive abilities are innate since they connect through energies in their environment. Free from ego, nothing is blocking the truth from being revealed in every moment.

Choose to live from the heart in the presence of animals. It will be easy to connect with them from a consciousness of the heart. Commune heart to heart. Choose to be loving, honoring, and assertive with your animals. They will feel safe and happy with you.

Teach your dog healthy guidelines and rules in fun and loving ways. You will both have a good time and a nice life together. Respect and love are the foundations to sustain harmony, joy, and wellness.

Your dog wishes to know what is expected from him. He likes when you are in charge, when you guide him and interact with him. Show him in kind and fun ways that you are in charge. Be gentle and clear, loving and confident. Do not show any aggressive behavior, but be assertive. Your dog is teaching you to be self-confident, aware, joyous, and grounded.

When communicating and interacting with animals, it needs to be understood that any form of mental or physical aggression alters the results of your wish to deeply connect since you are not coming from a place of love, respect, and harmony. Such energies create fears in animals. Work on communicating with feelings of pure love and from your heart with your environment and with all beings.

Your dog wishes to please you. Allow his best to be expressed. Create happy times and fun teachings. Uplift your energy and play with your dog. This is another way to invite and allow love's flow.

Animals feel and see what comes next because of their natural, clear way to experience oneness through vibrational frequencies, nature's intelligence, and nature's laws. Animals are energetically aware of multidimensional realms of consciousness within Mother Nature.

Animals feel agitated, anxious, and uneasy around human fear, cruelty, hatred, anger, or distress. Energies speak to them. When animals are abused, they experience stress, distress, and fear—they suffer.

The level of human unconsciousness is demonstrated and reflected in the proliferation of animal cruelty—and the killing of animals all around the world. Now is the time to awaken and stop this tragedy.

Animals sense your state of mind and thoughts; practice communicating with your animal friends through positive mental images and loving thoughts.
Animals teach us amazing ways to develop our creative abilities, self-confidence, joy, and inner awareness. They teach us to open our hearts. Seek help from a professional animal trainer and a certified spiritual practitioner if you need additional guidance and support for you and your pet. It will change your life in loving, empowering ways.

Learning to communicate with nature's intelligence on a deep level expands your consciousness as well as your love for all life. These are qualities you develop through time. Discover the beauty and sacredness of life with an open heart and with love. This journey of the heart will change your life in the most amazing ways. You will develop the ability to emanate qualities of love and wisdom in all circumstances and aspects of your life. It will increase your joy of living!

We contribute to harmonic evolution by demonstrating compassion and reverence, through the power of love, a consciousness of the heart.

Express love and joy with your animal friends. Have fun! Play with them! They will love to be around you. You will be surprised by their love and gifts. They are amazing companions. Open your heart. They live in the moment. They teach you how to live in the now, how to play in joy, and how to light up!

When humankind cut trees, destroys forests, or pollutes rivers and oceans, it jeopardizes all beings and all life. Diseases and abuse are then taking place, increasing the suffering of animals. What we do to the Earth and the animals, we do to ourselves.

Now is the time to live as enlightened beings.

ANIMALS, NATURE, AND FOOD

If you are truly wishing for harmony, happiness, and good health, you will effortlessly avoid eating foods and drinking substances with low vibrational life force—which are for the most part weakening your whole being. These are for the most part found in processed foods and genetically modified foods—trans fat oils, monosodium glutamate or MSG for short, artificial sweeteners such as aspartame, and various addictive substances. They are responsible for weight gain and create high levels of acidity in the physical body. Many of these products are potentially causing serious and sometimes fatal health problems.

We can all choose to create a better world together—one where all we create brings forth health, goodness, wellness, and harmony for all beings. Honor the Earth Being and life. Live with consciousness and help raising awareness.

> *In all of my conduct, I honor the harmonic flow of life and the beauty of Mother Earth. I choose to listen to the voice of Mother Earth. Every day, I learn about her sacredness. I am at peace with all life.*

If you embrace life with love, wish to feel good, and choose to evolve on your spiritual path, you will naturally be attracted to food with high vibrational life force.

The level of your vibrational life force frequency comes from the nature of your consciousness, how you live with your thoughts, feelings, intentions, and beliefs, how you respond to life and what you choose to eat.

Right now, you can choose to love yourself, despite your weight or anything you have been judging. Release all judgment. This is the beginning of your journey toward wellness and peace.

People have different missions and genetic programs—people respond to life and food in different ways.
It is important to find your own personal balance and eat what feels good and nurturing to your whole being—with consciousness.

If you choose to eat meat, be aware that many animals have been mistreated during their lives—before they end up in your plate, in your cellular structure and memory. Many of these beautiful creatures have suffered greatly, living in tremendous state of stress and distress, anxiety and fear—sometimes until the day they are killed.

Fear and stress create high levels of toxins. When we experience stress, we get sick because we create toxins in our physical bodies, blocking the life force, the love life flow in our cells and being. When animals endure distress and pain, that energy of fear creates tremendous levels of toxins in their tissues, blood, and whole body. Be aware that you also eat these toxic vibrations of pain and fear when you eat meat. Meat is of a much denser energy within your being than fruits and vegetables, and more difficult to digest.

When you proceed with a clearing and blessing prayer before you eat, it will release most of the toxicity or all of it, according to the way you pray. The energy of the animal's body needs as much love as the soul does, because of the fear and abuse the animal endured.

> *I ask that all vibrations of fear and pain embedded energetically within the cells, bodies, fields, and consciousness of this animal, be released into the divine light of God.* ***I ask that peace and harmony be restored in all time, space, and dimensions and be returned to the Earth Being with love and reverence.*** *And so it is. Thank you.*

Ask for infinite blessings of love, grace, and everlasting peace for this animal.

Pray with great compassion and love, asking for the soul of the animal to be completely, divinely assisted into the divine light, within its sacred realm. It will be a complete blessing. Express gratefulness.

It is always possible to express love and a sense of honoring that is healing to the world and to the animal kingdom.

Before you eat anything, choose thoughts of love and gratitude for the food life is providing. Ask God to bless your meal and water all the way to its source with infinite love, harmony and joy. Express gratefulness. Purify your food and water by raising the life force energy through prayers and thoughts of love, honoring, and gratitude.

When you eat with praise and consciousness, food becomes medicine love and light energy for your whole being. The love vibration of your prayers is always expanding and reaching all of creation, inviting more peace between all beings. It is the same for the food you give to animals—choose to express a blessing of love and gratitude before they eat their food. This nurturing, clearing energy supports their well-being and joy. My dog loves the energy.

If the people who prepared and touched your food had negative thoughts, were depressed, or angry, these vibrations are carried in this food. Make sure to change the vibrations of that meal. Your prayers and blessings will always energetically purify your food, increasing its life force and frequency. Ask for blessings of love and harmony for the people who have harvested, prepared, and touched this food.

Animals are assisting us greatly in our spiritual progress—and most people are not paying attention to their important and intrinsic role.

The considerable physical, mental, and emotional cruelties humans have been inflicting on animals have a negative impact on our lives and the life of Mother Earth. What we do to others, we always do to ourselves.
All the cruelty inflicted on animals is an energy that comes back to humankind in multiple ways—through illness, mental and emotional distress, and destructive behaviors—harming all levels and aspects of life.

Imagine all human beings as vegetarians. Or imagine humans taking the life of an animal for survival purposes, honoring the animal's life and soul through prayers. The quality of life for all beings would be tremendously enhanced. Mother Earth would also greatly benefit energetically from that shift in consciousness. The horrific slaughter of animals would come to an end. The wild horses would run free. Our natural environment, in general, would be more treasured. The percentage of illness would drop drastically. People would be healthier and happier.
Now is the time to awaken—a consciousness of the sacred has to prevail over greed and profit. Harmony for all life has to be treasured.

There was a time when Native Americans were asking permission with reverence and praise to the animal to be sacrificed—this was to serve their survival and basic needs. The soul of the animal and the physical body of the animal were honored and blessed. Originally, the Native Americans were sacrificing a limited number of animals based upon their immediate survival and needs. The animals were never mistreated. They knew how to live with consciousness and how to live the sacredness of life in praise and gratitude. Their way of living was beneficial to the physical body, the mind, and the soul, sustaining one's vital energy and emotional balance. They were honoring the Earth Being.

I encourage people to live mostly as vegetarians and to eat wide varieties of organic fruits and vegetables. Proteins are found in bee pollen, rice protein powder from whole grain sprouted brown rice, avocados, tofu, varieties of beans and nuts, almond milk, soy milk, and the like.

Bless the water you drink and ask that it remembers its original frequency. Everything has consciousness. Blessing food and water is nurturing for Mother Earth and all beings. It is another way to bring forth increasing peace and wellness for all beings, honoring the Earth Being. The power of love is forever omnipresent, omnipotent, and omniscient.

Communicate with Your Animal Friends with Awareness

The first time I met my dog, he recognized me and I recognized him, too. At four months old, when he arrived in my home with his brothers and sisters, he sat right away into the little bed I had prepared on the kitchen floor.

Later on, while observing his gracious walking body language I often had the vision of a black leopard. First, I was not sure from where these visions were coming from. I decided to explore our past lives together and one was clearly revealed to me. I was a medicine-women living in nature—it looked like a tropical forest—I was communing with nature's spirits and Mother Earth. One day I found an injured black baby leopard and healed his wounds with medicinal plants. As he was healing he was always free to go as he pleased but he never left my side—he became strong and powerful. He was protecting me and especially when I was sleeping—he was lying next to me. A few times I healed his wounds with medicinal plants—he was fighting off other animals to protect me. After witnessing this past life, I understood at a much deeper level our present connection and how to balance this energy in our present lives.

You may enjoy exploring why your animal companion is your life—it will most likely enrich your life.

Animals react in different ways to energies than humans do. Be attentive to the way they respond to energies—to keep you and them safe. Enjoy communing with their realm of consciousness, with love and reverence.

At this time, loads of pain and negative karmic issues are being released. Many animals are assisting in the release of these energies and many are in distress. Every being has a mission and purpose—in small ways and big ways—to give birth to a new world of peace and harmony. Goodness and love perpetuate in infinity.
It is crucial that we offer loving care to all animals whenever we have opportunities and means to do so.

It is an important time for all human beings to protect the animals. It is important that we sustain a consciousness of the sacred and learn to coexist in harmony, peace, and reverence.

In order to understand your animal friends, connect and bond with them from the heart. Fill your heart with so much joy and love energy. Slowly and gently, direct that energy into their heart center. Always proceed with reverence and loving-kindness. As you sustain your intent to communicate, visualize and experience a flow of love light energy between both of you—heart to heart. Animals embrace this loving energy. You will feel pure love emanating from their whole beingness because you have created a conscious connection and opened your heart to them.

You are able to communicate telepathically with your animal companions. Even if they are in the yard or another room, you will know what they need, what they are up to, and what they are asking for. They often come to you and show you. They know about your next step, your thoughts, your feelings, and your intentions. They receive information through waves of energy frequencies and images.

Learn to calm your mind. Open your heart and listen—you will feel what they feel. You will receive so much clarity about who they are and about their world. Ask them specific questions that are going to help you know them better. If you cannot receive their responses right away, keep practicing. You might receive feelings, perceive messages, or receive images in your mind.
You are learning to access additional and unfamiliar dimensional realms of reality. This expands your consciousness and opens your heart.

Always be open to the wonders of life, especially around your animal friends. You might develop a personal way to connect with them and know about their world—the Earth, our Mother.

Lovingly and joyfully explore the wonders of your world.

Witness their inner and outer beauty as your heart naturally communes with their heart on a very high note of love. There is a constant flow of love between you and them. Through love energies, animals are very open to communicating, having a playful time, and exchanging an unconditional flow of love.

Create and visualize beautiful sparkly pink light love ray energy in your heart. Gently and lovingly, direct that energy and ray all the way into the heart of your animal companion. Experience the love and communicate with love. Visualize a rainbow of light embracing you both throughout this communion.

Love light color vibrations represent sound waves and energy frequencies. A universal design of vibrational light color spectrums springs from all life and light. Rainbows source from light.

You have the ability to perceive, hear, feel, see, and discover forevermore the multidimensionality, beauty, and essence of life.

Your heart emanates a specific sound light love vibration that is unique to you. Animals have also specific sounds of light love vibration emerging from their hearts. You are both traveling on an energetic magnetic wave of love light sound and hues, communing with one another, heart to heart. With time, you will navigate in their worlds. Keep practicing. Open your heart to your magical world.

Communicating on such deep levels with animals is an extraordinary experience. Your friends are divine, sensitive beings. Such experience expands your ability to love and understand your animal friends and their realm at a very deep level. It expands your spiritual awareness about the wonders, beauty, and sacredness of your world.

Your animal friends are amazing teachers. They teach you to live in the now with joy and appreciation.

When we honor our animal friends and care for them with love and respect, the love they give back is multiplied and unconditional. Tell them how much you love them—and how happy and appreciative you are of them. Tell them how grateful you are that they are in your life. Tell them how beautiful and gentle they are, and how good they are. Ask questions about their favorite foods, where they like to sleep, and what they came to teach you. Learn about their mission and why they are in your life. Open your heart and listen. They are sacred beings—and you are too.

One day, I was driving very slowly on a mountain road, enjoying and breathing in all the beauty surrounding me. I suddenly stopped my car and opened the door slowly. As I was standing next to the car, about twenty-five feet away, four wolves were looking at me, sitting still. I was so surprised, but I stood still. I opened my heart, in awe, allowing love flow.

I felt safe, pure love consciousness—almost in a state of ecstasy. They were magnificent! I could observe an adult male and female and two younger wolves sitting on their side. We stood still, experiencing one another's energies of love, heart to heart, for about ten minutes. Then, very slowly, I entered my car, sending them unconditional love and energies of reverence. They were observing me calmly. As I slowly moved away, I felt as though I was being taken into higher realms of life and realities, or higher dimensions of life. It was truly magical and sacred.
It opened and expanded my heart and consciousness in ways I cannot describe.

Wonders Within the Aquatic Oceanic World

Water is for the Earth what blood is in our physical bodies. It covers about 71 percent of Earth's surface. The human body is composed of about the same amount of water. Water symbolizes purification and consciousness. Water has consciousness. It is an element of nature. Every element has consciousness working in harmonic synergy with all life.
It is so important to have loving, joyful thoughts when you are in contact with water, since water is infused with the frequency of thoughts, sound, and the nature of its environment. Energetic frequencies are vibrations traveling through water. Your thoughts are energies received by all life anytime and anywhere.

Water has its own consciousness and code, working in synergy with all sacred laws and divine design.
The original frequency of water has a high frequency of life force—in harmony with the Earth Being frequency. When we drink water at its original frequency, our bodies and field radiate with life force.

The polluted water on our planet reflects the human mind pollution, the ego, with all levels of unconsciousness.

Since it is no always easy to find pure water at its original frequency, I proceed with a blessing and prayer. Before drinking water, I sometimes check its life force. I bless it and add one or two drops of essential oils such as oregano or a few drops of fresh organic lemon juice. The life force rises substantially. Your blessings and prayers of love, as well as spiritual songs, music, and mantras bring forth the vibrational original quintessence of water. It also raises your vibrational frequency. All is energy and all is one.

> *Prayer for water: I ask for this water that the original frequency of its essence be awakened and activated in sacredness and love consciousness—within God's light. It is the water of light—the water of God. And so it is. Thank you.*

Water is energy consciousness—and energy is frequency and sound.
Sound travels four times faster through water since the molecular structure of water is denser.
When you are in contact with water or immersed in water, the nature of your emotions and thoughts are energetic vibrations that multiply and travel at very high speeds through water. They are received by all life forms within that realm and beyond.

When I swim, snorkel, or scuba dive in the ocean, I experience a new paradigm of consciousness, a limitless source of light energy, and cosmic consciousness. In the ocean, I feel an ancient, mystical side of life, a vast source of beauty, and a multitude of sacred worlds interconnecting within timeless space and countless intelligent forms of life.

All forms of life in water are evolving endlessly within timeless space and communing through sound-vibration frequencies, as all life is. The presence of the human race on Earth has created great distress within the aquatic ecological life. It is a time to live in reverence and respect all creation—we are one with all that is.

Every human being has to awaken and participate to life from a consciousness of the sacred, in reverence to all beings and all life.

When I swim in the ocean, I have tremendous fun bonding with all aquatic life, especially dolphin and whale energies. As I connect with the dolphins from my heart, a flow of joy moves through my whole being. I can experience that joy all the way into my heart and cells. I feel great exhilaration. I move in the water like a dolphin (with my snorkeling or scuba diving equipment). Naturally, effortlessly, I swim and dive deeper. My entire being feels playful, joyous, light, and free. I swim, experiencing the consciousness of a dolphin, and nothing else exists. I am transported within its consciousness, fully present in the moment. I experience the beautiful energies and multitudes of sounds within the oceanic realm. It is ecstatic. My consciousness is expanding limitlessly. My mind is free. My soul is free.

Bonding with dolphins, whales, and all marine life is an experience of love—a journey in the vastness of space. When I free dive or scuba dive, I always feel as if I am entering a limitless time and space reality—a magical realm of unlimited grace and beauty. I experience the sacredness of these mystical, majestic creatures. It is pure love, ecstasy, and joy.

Dolphins are very special to us. I see them as masters of light and great teachers of joy. A limitless source of love and joy emanates from them. Their free spirits and playful energies are a natural expression of their true essence—a boundless flow of joy. When that joy and harmony are shattered by humankind's inappropriate behavior, the soul cannot sustain its presence upon the Earth Being. Dolphins are then guided into higher worlds of light consciousness to sustain their true identities. This is what I have been told—and this has been my experience.

Dolphins are a gift to us from life, bringing forth and sustaining sacred spaces of high dimensions of light and joy for all beings to embrace.

When you communicate with them, they invite you to play within these high realms of joy consciousness. They guide you to discover who you truly are. They guide you to your source.

Similarly, whales are ancient, noble, and divine beings from faraway worlds. They hold true consciousness and wisdom. They have been the keepers of the mystical sacred treasures and mysteries of the world and humanity.

Their high state of consciousness is of infinite inner peace. They are teachers and masters of great ancient wisdom. Now is the time for all humans to learn to live from the heart, through the heart, honoring these beautiful holy creatures. Noble souls are waiting for you.

You have the ability to consciously commune with these extraordinary beings of the ocean—anytime and from anywhere. It is important to always connect in love and reverence. Listen to their messages; they lead you into realms of wonders and beauty.

It is about time that nobility, dignity, and sacredness for our animal friends are qualities that are understood and recognized. They lead us to the Garden of Eden of our sacred unified heart.

Loving and honoring all forms of life from all realms lead to global peace and harmony. The gift is to live in the true expression and consciousness of our beingness. We then truly "see", honor, and love all beings.

CHAPTER SIX

Understanding our Relationship with the Spirit World and the Physical World—the Invisible and the Visible

THERE IS NO SEPARATION BETWEEN **the inner world and the outer world. All is one—all is connected.**

In this chapter, I intend to specifically address humankind's relationship with all of creation in regard to the spirit world and the world of physicality (the mind and heart of the Cosmos—the mind and heart of God), the unseen, and the seen, and how they work and interact in absolute oneness.

THE INVISIBLE AND THE VISIBLE AND THE TREE OF LIFE

The flow of divine creative life force throughout all of creation is in perpetual transcendence, encompassing the invisible and the visible, all laws and cosmic realms, all realms of existence and aspects of life—living within the Tree of Knowledge and the Tree of Life—the mind of God and the heart of God.

The Tree of Knowledge (the invisible) and the Tree of Life (the visible) hold the conduit and bridge between the unmanifested and the manifested, between the invisible and the visible. When the mind works through the heart there is unity consciousness—we then live from Spirit, from the soul consciousness.
The unmanifested is of pure formless consciousness and divine knowledge—the mind of God. Spirit is the source from which creative energetic manifestation emerges to come into physical expression and existence. Energy comes into form when activated by various energetic frequencies. From Spirit springs all life.

When we fully recognize the highest power of love from the Creator sourcing from all creation, we surrender to it and live it—there is an illumination of the hearts. The sun of the high heart fuses with the sun of the heart chakra anahata, revealing unity consciousness. **The Tree of Life is then awakening and naturally filled with true divine knowledge.**
We then experience oneness as a holy force in consciousness.

When there is an illumination of the unified heart illuminating the mind, the true nature of the Tree of Knowledge and the Tree of Life are revealed as one divine life force and flow—the mind and the heart of God are experienced. We then experience our wholeness and true divine nature.
This process comes into action when the force of love and light of the divine masculine invites in harmony the nurturing force of love, grace, and light of the divine feminine. Our whole beingness is unified through the central essence of our holy nature—revealing the God-Self. We are experiencing the consciousness of God. The Garden of Eden is revealed on Mother Earth, into our hearts, and in all life. Heaven is invited on Earth. The Earth Being is celebrating with joy.

The Tree of Life is bridging the Sky or Heaven with the Earth

Being, within its vertical ascensional path, guiding one's creative journey and expression from the invisible to the visible, and from the visible to the invisible realms. We have the ability to live within a unified field of consciousness, navigating through all realms from one true consciousness of the illuminated heart.

There is a divine cosmic design, which embodies all creation extending throughout the universe, encompassing all souls and forms of life—and from which all forms and activities emanate on the planes of manifestation. There is an energetic flow of frequencies and harmonic synergies amid the visible and the invisible forever creating.

True Power of Love in Your Inner and Outer World

When you wake up, make a deliberate decision to raise your vibrations by honoring "you" and honoring all life through nurturing feelings of gratefulness and love in your heart. When you wake up, move into a state of peaceful meditation for a few minutes. Start your day contemplating the world with renewed awareness, thoughtfulness of appreciation, and sacredness.

Honoring life is experiencing a profound state of praise, reverence, and sacredness in every moment of your existence. It is an experience of love. It is appreciating and revering the people in your life with your animal companions, the trees, the flowers, the wind, the sun, the rain, and all that is in your world. Glorify all that is. In such conscious space, you are in harmonic symbiosis and synergy with the physical-material world and the spirit world. You have the possibility to explore all of its magic and beauty. You are an empowered being.

An empowered being reveres and praises all of life, holding deep love and respect for the Earth Being and all its inhabitants. An empowered being nurtures and empowers others. An empowered being knows how to receive with love and knows how to give with love. An empowered being lives from the heart and knows truth.

An empowered being naturally shows humility and compassion. An empowered being is always forgiving, living with consciousness in feelings, thoughts, and actions. An empowered being is listening, speaking, breathing, and living from the heart. An empowered being lives in joy and gratitude and brings loving-kindness into the world.

When you open your eyes in the morning, tell yourself that every breath, every move, and every moment holds the beauty, love, and grace of God. Relishing in that realization leads to a sense of unity and bliss. It becomes a way of life, harmoniously supporting the manifesting creative process within your inner world and outer world.

In every moment, from your beingness flows a magnetic energy in action—a frequency that you allow and create in the invisible and bring forth into the visible. You emanate and create specific frequencies or waves of consciousness in every moment. They manifest within the physical world and in your life.

When you allow the divine qualities of the essence of life to awaken from the core of your being, you are forever creating from that blissful infinite emanation, to serve all of life's highest purposes.

The divine qualities of God embedded within the essence of life encompass the sacred codes and design of the Flower of Life and the Tree of Life. All divine designs belong to the creation—they belong to God.

If you live from the ego, all your thoughts are running your life. You create from a lower vibration that does not express and convey harmony, joy, and goodness. You feel pain and aloneness. You have invited chaotic energies that are shattering your beingness and your interaction within both worlds.

The inner world or spirit (the invisible) is where light energy consciousness flows boundlessly. When our thoughts, feelings, and intentions are frequencies from the heart, we experience a divine flow, wholeness, and happiness. We are then honoring our divine design and oneness. There is one frequency of peace love light and harmony that we invite in the visible, physical world.

Our global structural field of light is now being renewed and reprogrammed to ensure global transcendence, toward higher frequencies of light. The Tree of Life is revealed within its new polarities. Our whole world—inner and outer—is being upgraded, reprogrammed, transformed, and adjusted to match the energies of peace love light—of the fifth dimension. This process unifies all hearts to the "central heart"—the heart of all hearts—in one radiant light. It is the heart of God.

Your whole being and every cell have intelligence, and are supported by a magnetic field of light frequencies. When you choose to live from the heart you allow peace love light flow. This flow and force emanate from the core essence of life. This force lives in you.

Your cells, DNA, and RNA are infused with increasing light and life force the moment you embrace compassion, reverence, and love.

Learn to navigate with grace and in sacred ways between your inner and outer world—between the visible and the invisible. Live in the oneness of your being.

As you learn to navigate in harmony between the visible and the invisible, you will know your oneness within both worlds. You will recognize and witness the energy-flow bridging the physical/material plane, and the spirit/soul plane as one love light synergy.
You will experience an awareness of the mind through the heart that holds your faith and love. The ego fades away.
Nothing limits the creative flow of your heart's desires. Your creative possibilities and potentialities are limitless—all is energy.

This book is guiding you to walk through all twelve doorways of light. These twelve doorways of light represent the divine qualities of God anchored in your illuminated heart and mind. They are sourcing from the heart and mind of God—bringing forth the divine feminine aspect of God, guiding you to the ultimate portal of light—the portal to your God-Self.

WHO ARE YOU WITHIN THE INVISIBLE AND THE VISIBLE?

Many people have a tendency to identify with what they have or with their professional achievements instead of recognizing the true and divine aspect of their being and existence. It is important to feel grateful and be appreciative for all that life is giving you from a consciousness of the heart and to live in the joy of your divine presence.

When you identify obsessively with what you have on a material level or what you have achieved, you are not in touch with your inner being. You are ignoring some fundamental aspects of your beingness. It is important to find grace and balance, appreciation and gratefulness in the oneness of all realms and aspects of life.

If you dwell upon feelings of insecurity, frustrations, restlessness, jealousy, or greed, your ego is in charge and you have lost your balance. In that space, you are limiting yourself, ignoring the fundamental aspect of your being.

If you forget who you are, you are moving away from your life's purpose and happiness. Your possessions or accomplishments will never seem satisfactory. There will always be something missing that is fundamental to your wholeness and happiness—you have been looking for this missing part in the wrong places, forgetting who you are. Open your heart and bring forth love and goodness in everything you do. You will feel whole and happy.

Learn to enjoy life and all that life is offering with consciousness. Rest in the peace and bliss of your inner presence from a place of gratitude. Blissful serenity is born from within.

Discover who you are all the way to the heart of your soul—and then live it fully in joy!

Your soul belongs to the invisible spirit world—Spirit—God. The foundation of your life consciousness and experience starts within the spirit world from the heart of your soul—from God—and extends into physicality.

Be a Bridge of Love

If well managed or equitably allocated, there is an abundance of food available for every living being today. How is it possible that there are staggering numbers of people who have no homes and are going hungry every day? It is reported that there are about 2 billion hungry and undernourished people in the world today. There are about 7 billion people in the world. How can this be? We have the ability to awaken and to resolve together these issues.

Now is the time for all human beings and all nations to come together and truly see one another from an awakened heart. Now is the time for every human being to come into the realization that we are one global family programmed to live in unity consciousness. Life is a divine design of love light consciousness encompassing all beings and all life.

I am living as a conscious light being, creating bridges of love light shining in all directions of the globe.

Now is the time for all qualities of compassion to awaken from the heart of every human being, to heal all wounds on all levels of existence.

I would like to share with you the following quote from Mother Teresa, an excerpt from the book: The Authorized Biography by Navin Chawla. "There are thousands of lonely people, living by themselves, not necessarily physically poor, but poor in ways that Mother says are worse than in Calcutta.

She says the spiritual poverty of the West is far greater than the physical poverty of the so-called developing countries.

She calls these unwanted people the "shut-ins." It is far harder to cure that form of loneliness. These people are "nobody." Nobody notices them. Some of the people whom few care to notice live in a veritable township of cardboard boxes, huddled under Waterloo Bridge, in parks such as Lincoln's Inn Fields and near London's underground stations. Home is a cardboard box a little larger than a coffin. It is often their only protection against the icy winds of winter. For most of them, the only genuine smiles they receive are from the sisters and co-workers. On two nights a week, beginning about 10:00 p.m., an ambulant soup kitchen brings them a hot meal. With this come words of cheer and sounds of laughter."

Warfare, hatred, inequality, and poverty come from greed, bigotry, and ultimately fear. Unconsciousness brings about fear. The ego is gladly entertaining chronic fears born from illusory beliefs and distorted views of the world.

The ego is often in charge when there is a lack of inner spiritual search and contemplation. The ego is in charge when there is a lack of connective awareness with one's divinity and soul's purpose. This is why so many children are mistreated, in pain, neglected, or abandoned. This is why many people fear one another. This is why so many people are going hungry every day. This is why so many animals are mistreated and are suffering. This is why there are wars.

As long as people fear one another, peace cannot prevail.

Life is providing endlessly for all beings. It is for all human beings to see and honor one another, to honor the Earth Being, all of creation, and its amazing beauty and boundless gifts of love. It is for all human beings to awaken and love one another. Be that bridge of love!

I like and appreciate this quote from screen actor Sidney Poitier: *"Every day I try to be a better person than I was yesterday so that when I die I will not be afraid to have lived."*

Heart Soul Connective Awareness with the Earth Being and the Cosmos

In reverence, I praise Mother Earth's astounding beauty. I live within an extraordinary symbiosis of nurturing love consciousness in perfect synergy and oneness with the divine laws of nature, encompassing all creation. I am loved and cared for, forever held in God's sempiternal radiance.

Humankind has often abused Mother Earth's precious and sacred resources, often in manners of greed and for personal gain, resulting in suffering for all beings. Polluting the earth and the oceans—poisoning food and water—spraying poisons on crops, around homes, parks and playgrounds are behaviors born from ignorance or unconsciousness, jeopardizing all natural laws and flow of life—our global ecosystem.

Such behaviors are infringing to the sacredness of life, its divine design, and harmonic synergy, causing all kinds of illness—mental and physical suffering. Thousands of animal species and forms of life are becoming extinct.

Now is the time for all human beings to awaken to their true purpose and spirituality.

Life is forever supportive and loving—we live it when we choose to express the qualities of the heart and the soul. In order to live in that reality and synergy—compassion, reverence, and love are required from you, from me, and from every human being. We have to live in these same frequencies of the heart together, as one family.

The global energetic geometrical light grid holds all life's codes and intelligent light patterns. It holds all sacred geometry of light from which all life is sourcing.

It is a sacred design of the highest vibrations of peace love light. This divine design operates in harmonic oneness with all sacred laws encompassing all aspects and qualities of God. Its full source of light is revealed through an activation of the Tree of Life—revealing the Flower of Life.

The Flower of Life is an intelligent blueprint and sacred design embedded within all life and emanating from all creation, encompassing the Tree of Life and all sacred geometry. All sacred geometry including the Tree of Life has its source in the heart of creation. It belongs to the creation.
When the unified sacred heart is enlightened to express unity consciousness, the Tree of Life is revealed in its wholeness—and your light body shines. Light springs from your heart and illumines your mind to know true consciousness. Your heart is a sun shining its rays, revealing the qualities of the soul.

All of life's energetic and magnetic structures are now being upgraded to embrace with ease higher dimensions of light. Our God-Self is being activated within a new vibrational frequency. In order to fully embrace that activation we have to embrace the qualities of the heart to invite and allow enlightenment.

Embracing the sacredness in all life is living with consciousness, connecting with the multidimensionality of your being—God's consciousness—nature's consciousness. You naturally progress toward the full realization of your God-Self, oneness, and wholeness.

From the consciousness of your soul and heart, commune with Mother Earth in honoring—learn to live in harmonic synergy with the Earth Being—heart to heart. Invite with gratitude her nurturing love in your heart, in your whole beingness and in your life. Mother Earth is healing you. Mother Earth is forever nurturing you.
(Please view the meditation at the end of chapter four, The Tree of Life • A Portal to Your God-Self.)

When we make peace within and with all life, divine alignment occurs—within all dimensions and planes of our experience and beingness—we invite peace on Earth.

Bring forth your magic wand of love. Use it to create joy in your life and in the lives of others. You are the magician and your wand is love. Learn to live heart to heart. Learn to receive and embrace all the gifts of boundless love emanating from the heart of all creation.
Learn to receive from God.
From the heart of the Galaxy, from the heart of the Cosmos—from the heart of the Heavens—from the heart of Mother Earth and from your enlightened heart and mind miracles are born from love—from the one heart and mind of God.

God's consciousness is intrinsic to all life and creation—it is a holy source and essence of infinite divine knowledge and unconditional love. It is the essence of life.

From the heart of creation we receive boundless gifts of love.

A PATH TO BLISS

There are people throughout the world—known or unknown, from all social backgrounds, in all countries—who are dedicated to serve all beings and all life—doing God's work.
There are beautiful souls throughout the planet who are contributing to wellness, goodness, and harmony for all beings. These light workers are uplifting the whole world. You are one of them—this is why you are reading this book.
Whatever you do out of love every day has a ripple effect—even if you don't realize it. You are helping the world be a better place.

You don't need to be famous or rich to be happy and to be of service—all you have to do is "love". Allow your whole beingness to be infused with love. When love flows, all flows in harmony.

Listen to your children. They are still very connected to the spirit world during their early years. They remember their divinity. They know about their most natural way of being and your most natural way of being.

You have the ability to remember who you are too. You can be that child again and remember—by freeing your mind from all indoctrination and thought forms. Learn to focus on your sacredness and beauty—and rediscover the true being of love you are in every moment of your existence.

I have met people who were attached to so many "things" that they were in a continuous state of turmoil and anxiety. It is good to gently guide and help these people comprehend that they are not all these materiel things. They are eternal, beautiful, multidimensional divine light beings ready to express higher purposes. The real vastness and richness of their God-Self and true divine knowledge is far greater than all they have ever had and known from these material possessions.

When they know who they are they will then appreciate and enjoy all of life—in harmony.

True divine knowledge is sourcing from the heart of my soul, activated by the illuminated mind—God consciousness living in me.
Every day, I learn to receive boundless nurturing gifts of love from God. Life is forever nurturing me.

BREATHING WITH CONSCIOUSNESS IS INVITING INCREASING LIFE FORCE AND JOY

The action of breathing creates an interplaying link and synergy between the physical and spirit world. In Greek, breath means "Spiritus or Spirit". Breath is Spirit, wind, life force or prana. The meaning of "breathing and breath" is living from Spirit—from God—in consciousness of the soul and of the life force.

Meditating from a consciousness of the breath is guiding you to the discovery of your true identity. Meditating while focusing of the breath brings you strength, awareness, courage, balance and good health—it guides you to true consciousness. You are anchoring in love light life force. You are anchoring in your essence.

I think of the breath as an interplaying link of light energy in action—uniting the visible and the invisible. It is a life force in action living in me and nurturing me. When you live in consciousness of your breathing patterns and practice diverse breathing exercises, you naturally bring increasing life force into your cells, your whole physical envelope, and whole beingness. This increasing life force is nourishing your physical body and whole being with Spirit, with light, with life, and with love. This process strengthens the mind and personality to operate from the heart, leading to the illuminated one mind and heart consciousness.

Breathing is life force energy. It is an aspect of Spirit sustaining you in love.

If your breath is shallow, you are most likely depleted of life force—your life force is low.
As you calm the mind, connect with the life force energy in your breathing. Feel the energy of your breathing moving through your whole being all the way to your cells, nurturing you and loving you.

Learn to become conscious of the life force through therapeutic breathing exercises. As you build up your life force or chi, you have the ability to heal anxiety, depression, fear, and illness in the physical body. Since you are inviting further light and life force into your space and beingness you are also clearing your whole space.

Work on deepening your breath. Learn to become fully conscious of your breath. Every day, practice deep and slow breathing—expand your magnetism of light in the consciousness of your breathing. In every breath, feel and relax every part of your body.

Breathe for a longer time and deeper—in areas of your body that are tense.

I am relaxing, relaxing, relaxing. I breathe peace love light force.

Repeat these words, until you feel your whole beingness relaxing. Breathing with consciousness is nurturing and calming. Experience your whole being relaxing, breathing love light life force. As you practice, it becomes easier to invite wellness and peace—further inviting you to live within the consciousness of your divine presence.

There are many breathing techniques you may wish to practice and learn. They activate the energy flow within your whole being. You have the possibility to practice breathing techniques in yoga, martial arts, and spiritual practice, and attending respiratory therapy classes or breathing schools. Hiking, running, and swimming activate your breathing. They all enhance your energetic flow in wonderful ways, increasing your life force and balance.

Therapeutic breathing releases blocked energies and recharges you with life force. It balances the mind or mental body, your emotional body, and all your bodies. It activates your light body and leads you to clarity and serenity.

Breathing with consciousness is breathing with God and in God. It is of God.

My breath is the breath of God!

Your greatest contribution to life is sourcing from the heart—it is your willingness to love and allowing yourself to be loved by all life. Conscious breathing supports your well-being and your journey to be a blessing of love to all life. You are receiving boundless gifts of love.

CHAPTER SEVEN

Personal—Global Awareness
and Transcendence
• Light and Darkness •
Insights about Today's Energies

WHAT IS LIGHT? - WHAT IS DARKNESS?

B ASED UPON ALL PREVIOUS INSIGHTS, I wish to introduce a greater understanding of what is called the light and of what is called the darkness. This relates to multiple aspects of our existence and life's purpose. Many people have asked me questions about this vast topic.

Many cultures and traditions speak of the union of two polarized forces, the yang and yin, the masculine and feminine principles, the source of the light or white light and the source of darkness or dark light, the "Spiritual Sun or Father Sky, above" and the "Mother of Life or Earth Mother, beneath," the visible and the invisible, the seen and unseen, day and night, matter and spirit encompassing all spiritual and sacred laws—two forces united in one force—a divine design bringing into existence all of creation manifested.

These two forces represent two compatible energies encompassing all sacred laws and synergies of life. Life and death are one, as a continuum of expressed "force and energy consciousness" in action.
What most people call death is a transitional time for the soul to move on to a new journey, leaving behind a physical body that is no longer needed. You are eternally consciousness.

Heaven and Earth united through the vertical axis, or trunk, of the Tree of Life and Knowledge connects all the planes of the underworld of the terrestrial world with the celestial world, encompassing all four directions in a synergy of oneness. All six directions (North, East, South, West, above, and below) are sourcing from the center of creation or heart of creation—we can name it the seventh direction. This design and synergy is anchored within every human being and in all life. Creation begins at the heart. The embryo's heart is the first organ that comes into form. It is the portal of the soul, the sacred source of divine love.

It is possible to look upon these two forces, light and darkness, as different expressions of the same essence, interacting and also uniting in one force of light.
In some traditions or cultures, the darkness is recognized as the "light of the dark," and light is recognized as the "white light."

I personally look at the white light and the black light as two aspects of the light, and see that in reality there is one divine light consciousness and design from which all of creation is sourcing.

The white light and the black light (from each of which energy flows) liberate multitudes of color spectrums, magnetic fields, and electric fields, characterized by multitudes of wavelengths—energies and frequencies—interacting and navigating throughout all life and creation.

In spiral motion, light abides by the sacred laws in perfect synergy, serving all of life's purpose. There is no beginning and no end within the laws, within all of creation—light and space operate within the same continuum and spectrum of realities. It is infinity.

Our world is in existence within the interaction of different expressions of light, also representing one energetic force, inherently embedded in the expression of all life. The white light and the black light complement one another. They work in unison in the oneness of the cosmic heart.

There is a unification of forces and energies throughout all of life, inviting oneness—unity consciousness. We ultimately recognize one sacred and supreme light.

Our global shift invites all forces to come together in oneness, illuminating the heart and the mind. Love is the heart of that sacred union and unification of forces.

Different Aspects of What is Called Darkness

Chronic fears, destructive behaviors and beliefs are activating an energetic veil, holding one's inability to see truth leading to depression, illness, pain, and suffering. Sometimes people call this state of being a state of darkness—as an inability to truly love, to receive love, to see truth, to see the light, and be aware of the Higher Self or God-Self. We can see how darkness is serving light, since it is from that darkness that light emerges the moment the person awakens and opens the heart. We can see that from the dark light the white light emerges. All is one and all is consciousness. All is light!

In this situation what is called "darkness" is a place of suffering. It is ignoring the fundamental aspects of one's being. It is ignoring the qualities of the soul and the heart. It is ignoring one's God-Self. Such darkness is a state of consciousness created by thoughts and beliefs. It is an illusory state. When the heart opens, darkness is transmuted into love consciousness and divine qualities.

There is grace and love light beneath all suffering. Many humans learn and grow from pain. This pain leads to greater compassion, opening the heart to greater abilities to love. This is why beneath all darkness or suffering there is tremendous peace love light and grace. The intrinsic beauty of the soul is ready to shine in love at any moment.

You don't need to experience pain to embrace love, harmony, and true consciousness. You have the ability to live within the consciousness of your Higher Self right now. You can choose to awaken to your divine qualities and love all life right now!

People often say that there is a lot of darkness in this world. They complain and express anger and frustration, and sometimes hatred. Anger, frustration, and hatred are energies feeding the same energies they wish to see eradicated. In reality, and without knowing it, they are feeding the exact same energy they are labeling as dark. Probably, we have all expressed frustrations about this matter at a time or another. It is good to remember and realize that true power is the power of love.

Judging and dwelling to negativity are feeding dark energies. It is important to become aware of the presence of love and light underneath that "darkness".
Learn to live your life free from judgment and open your heart in compassion and love. Contribute to goodness and peace. Live your purpose. Raise awareness through love and in love! Shine your light!

Every time you see injustice, pain, and suffering, choose to hold love and compassion in your heart. See how you can bring awareness and goodness into the world from a place of reverence, harmony, and unconditional love.

To feel separated from the Divine—from God—is very painful to the soul. The good news is that we are never separated from God. God is within us as a divine design of peace love light consciousness,

a supreme life force of unconditional love, intrinsically embedded in the core essence and heart of our being—within all forms and life. It is our choice to live within the consciousness of our true nature.

All life is fluid light energy!

Within all darkness, there is grace, love, and light. It is for every being to learn to "see" in the dark—to see the light!

Inviting Heaven on Earth Through the Heart

Compulsive, negative, destructive thought forms, words, and behaviors are a form of enslavement. It is similar to being unconscious. These negative energies are reinforcing a false reality and a fragmentary vision of life, creating struggle and confusion.

Responding to any kind of hostility with similar hostile energies emphasizes the cycle of violence, misery, and suffering. But responding with forgiveness, and compassion, creates a shift. It awakens and unifies all hearts. It is from a consciousness of the heart that hostility is transformed into compassion and love.

Grace emanates from forgiveness. It dissolves any hostile energy and uplifts all consciousness. There is nothing to fight for any longer. Compassion, tolerance, understanding, and reverence prevail. **Living in the power of love is awareness and wisdom. It is living in the light of your divine essence and the heart of your soul. It is living in the oneness of the heart. It is living Heaven on Earth.**

There are two contradictory forces experienced. One is made of pain fed by illusory thoughts or ego, pulling you away from who you are. The other one is of pure love, reveling in your divinity. One leads to chaos and misery, and the other leads to blissful serenity, love, and joy. One is a world of illusion and confusion, and the other one is of true consciousness, love, and peace.

Moving into true consciousness is experiencing a deeper activation of our divine design.

We do not have to steal anything in order to receive what we wish for—on all levels and aspects of our existence. We have the ability to receive in harmony everything we need without forcing, stealing, betraying, and hurting. In fact, taking from others by those means brings forth negative consequences (or negative karma), which create fears, insecurity, misery, and disharmony on all levels of someone's life. You live and experience the frequency and nature of the energy you project; it is the law of karma.

Every human being is divinely guided toward the realization of his or her true divine identity.

Close your eyes and imagine that your world is a friendly place, completely safe, forever supportive and loving in all ways. Meditate on this "reality" as often as you can. Experience the energy of serenity, bliss, and happiness as an undeniable reality.

The mind has the ability to recognize the path of the heart and walk within its consciousness. All separation (pain) is transmuted into oneness, wholeness, and unconditional love.

You have the ability to be an instrument of light.
I am light. I breathe peace love light in my heart and invite God's light in my space. The peace love light of God permeates my whole being and space. In my unified heart I visualize a golden white sun radiating light. I direct one ray of this radiant light through all my chakras (energy centers) and spinal column, all the way to the heart of the Earth Being. I experience the nurturing love of Mother Earth.
I travel on this ray of light back into the light of my heart. I expand this ray all the way to the heart of the Heavens. I experience its infinite divine consciousness. I now see myself as a ray of golden white light and I bask in that energy.
Slowly, I come back in the space of my energy field and physical body. I breathe

this sacred light energy in all my bodies and energy field. I have opened a flow of boundless peace love light, divine guidance, and nurturing healing energies.

Be aware of the peace love light in your space and in your whole energy field. Experience the healing nurturing energies. Your energy field encompasses your body of light, your physical body, a space around you, above, and below. Stay aware of the energy flow of love nurturing your physical body and your whole beingness. Your mind is at peace—you are receiving infinite gifts of love. Enjoy the experience of receiving and express deep gratitude.

Your unified heart is illuminated with love and is illuminating your mind. You have opened the portal to your God-Self. You are experiencing the heart and mind of God. It is a consciousness inviting Heaven on Earth. This divine union reveals the Garden of Eden and the Tree of Life within you and in all life—God consciousness within you and in all life.

I choose to live Heaven on Earth within and without.
I live in the Garden of Eden of my heart.

POLITICAL INDOCTRINATION

Destructive political characteristics, ongoing mental indoctrination of the population, inducing fear and hatred among nations and people from all faiths, and perpetuating inequality for personal gain comes from unconsciousness. Such illusory beliefs demonstrate a lack of awareness about the sacredness of life. Such political attributes are the source of hostility, prejudice, violence, and great suffering. Such destructive behaviors represent a matrix of energy generating warfare, illness, and poverty on the planet.

Can you see the detrimental consequences of participating to such antagonistic political indoctrination in your life, for the planet, and in all life?

I see that the true leaders of the world—and true conscious people—have integrity. They never dwell on violence and warfare. They inspire people to love and revere all beings and all life. They encourage people to learn from one another in beneficial ways. They bring forth a wisdom that is from the heart. They use all resources for the goodness of all people and all beings—for education, environmentally safe new technologies, equitable food and resource distribution.

Through these words, I wish to bring forth an awareness of the soul for all beings to choose a path where all qualities of love are expressed so that global peace and harmony prevail. May all hearts open in love! My purpose is to bring forth an experience of the God-Self, revering all beings and all life.

You have the free will, the choice, and the ability to step outside of all human thought forms and connect with your inner being of unconditional love.

The truth is that everyone wants to live in peace!
Everyone wants to be happy, feel safe, and loved.

Indoctrinated by political leaders, the media induces people to believe that engaging in warfare is about serving their country and keeping their families safe. These young men and women are being persuaded and indoctrinated that it is all right to kill their so-called enemies—and if these enemies are eliminated, they will be able to live in peace. In reality, this is when all hell starts.

In warfare, a profound state of distress, fear, and pain invades the innermost part of our brothers and sisters. It is caused by feelings of inner separation with their true divine nature—their God-Self. That separation is painful because they feel forced to ignore their true divine identity to be able to partake in such violence. It is a violation of their being. Inducing people to engage in warfare is a violation of one's being and a violation of all life. It is a violation of the sacredness of life.

When returning back from warfare, profound states of distress, fear, and pain persist within their mental and emotional bodies, and within the memory of the cells. They remain within people's bodies and consciousness—unless deep and thorough inner spiritual healing is being initiated and pursued daily.

It takes strong willingness and faith to overcome and let go of traumas caused by wars, but it is possible to overcome about everything through surrendering, compassion, and love. When returning to their homes and families, these men and women experience anxiety, depression, and nightmares. It is a state of distress, which often creates chaos in their lives and families.

Deep emotional pain often last an entire lifetime—unless their souls commit to completely reconciling with life, by embracing appropriate spiritual counseling, support, and spiritual practice.

We all need to come together to help, offer our support, and hold great love in our hearts for these beautiful souls and their families. We have to express compassionate love from our hearts and help these men and women find comforting feelings and peace—so they gently receive the inner guidance to return home within themselves, experiencing their God-Self.

Children naturally take on emotions from their parents. Children are naturally very open toward people they love, people who love them, and people who take care of them. Therefore, they take on love as well as pain.

If you wish to contribute to a better world, stop listening to the mass media and fiery, manipulative political rhetoric. Spend more time in meditation and focus on your true purpose and mission. You will be surprised by what is revealed to you. By consciously sustaining the sacredness of your space, your wholeness, and your integrity, you are opening a space of peace and well-being. **Your mind becomes free from all mental pollution. You are actually inviting true knowledge and the experience of an enlightened creative mind.**

Learn to have awareness over the energies you are allowing in your space. No one can perturb your inner peace unless you consent to it.

Place yourself in God's hands, love, and light. Surrender in the most challenging situations and in the most glorious moments. You can choose to live as a conscious being in every moment of your existence. Connect with the heart of your soul—delve into the most sacred aspect of your beingness. Nothing and no one can take your divinity or God-Self away from you—it is your essence of light. You are whole and holy.

Now is the time to come together with great love and compassion. It is important to forgive and love one another. As we commune heart to heart, we sustain a global sacred space—we embrace peace and unity consciousness in love.

Now is the time to see one another. Now is the time to love one another.

AWARENESS ABOUT TODAY'S ENERGIES

Through mercy, compassion, grace, and love, know that you have the power to inspire, uplift, transform, and harmonize. If you live from your heart, you have activated a spiritual power to open other people's hearts. Choose to be a source of goodness and bliss to all life.

Mother Earth provides boundless resources for all beings, but today more than 15 million children die of hunger, malnutrition, and poverty every year. All this suffering is a projection of a global consciousness, lacking awareness, mercy, and love.
Please join me in holding the vision and prayer for all the people of the world to unite as messengers of peace, to exude compassionate love for one another and to revere all beings!
It is crucial that we unite as a human family and choose to participate in a new Earth as emissaries of peace, compassion, reverence, love, and light.

Many light workers from all realms are coming together to invite and activate an infinite flow of peace love light all around the world—and where it is needed the most.

You have the choice and the ability to consciously contribute to goodness—and to work with all light workers—as one force of love. Choose to be an emissary of peace. Your foundation is in your heart. Love all beings and the Earth, our Mother. She is nurturing us and embracing us with love.

In order to bring an end to a chain of suffering, misery, and violence, it is necessary to raise our consciousness to the realization that it is only through "love" that we bring back anyone to "love"— despite any exterior circumstances.

Forgiveness, mercy, and compassion activate a powerful frequency of love, guiding all hearts to awaken. Love heals all wounded hearts and all wounded egos!
Responding to violence, corruption, and bigotry with similar negative destructive energies is giving power to those negative patterns and energies. This is why and how misery is being perpetuated. It is contributing to the very thing you would like to eradicate—or see eradicated.

Carl Jung said, "Until you make the unconscious conscious, it will direct your life and you will call it fate."

It is our duty to lovingly uplift and help one another from the heart and place our focus and efforts on working toward a world of tolerance, equality, and peace—together.

What Buddha said many years ago holds true today: "Do not believe in anything simply because you have heard it. Do not believe in anything simply because it is spoken and rumored by many. Do not believe in anything simply because it is found written in your religious books. Do not believe in anything merely on the authority of your teachers and elders. Do not believe in traditions because they have been handed down for many generations. But after observation and analysis, when you find that anything agrees with reason and is conducive to the good and benefit of one and all, then accept it and live up to it. It is fearlessness, and it is love."

CHAPTER EIGHT

Connect with Infinite Divine Creativity through the Discovery of Your Purpose and Mission

We discover who we are after we make peace within.
We receive clarity when we forgive and make peace with all life.
We feel whole and happy when we live within the consciousness of our true essence.
All the blessings of life are revealed to us when we experience bliss and serenity.
When love and light flow we invite divine creativity— purpose and mission are revealed.

PURPOSE AND MISSION

WHEN BIRTHING WITHIN THE PHYSICAL realm, every being is crossing the threshold with mission and purpose.

You have chosen to reincarnate in this physical body with a mission—to bring about a higher purpose and participating through your God-given gifts to the harmony and beauty in all life. It is a journey of discovery about your sacredness and the sacredness in all life.

In order to understand your mission and purpose learn to live in energetic alignment with your God-Self—learn to live every day within that consciousness. Allow your calling to be revealed by opening your heart to be loved by all life and to love all life!

> *I lovingly allow myself to awaken to the gifts of love and beauty permeating my whole being.*
>
> *I emanate all qualities of God's consciousness. It is a boundless flow of "unconditional love and divine knowledge". I choose to serve the light sourcing from all life—in that "love and divine consciousness".*
>
> *God's love consciousness permeates my whole beingness. I experience unconditional love, blissful serenity, and joy. I choose to be a blessing of unconditional love to all beings and all life.*

If deep feelings of emptiness are invading your inner space, if there is an increasing longing for love, peace, and oneness, or if the call for making a difference is in your thoughts, you are ready for a major shift of consciousness. It is a time to fill this emptiness with God's love. It is a space in which you gently adjust your whole being to new energies. As you are invited and initiated into realms of pure love, you are discovering who you are. Your purpose and mission are naturally revealed to you as you reconcile with life.

As you discover the true nature of your purpose and mission, your heart's desire is to create in divine ways—as the ultimate expression of love to serve God.

> *I lovingly open my heart to accept infinite love and grace— this energy permeates my whole being and life! Gratitude is my prayer.*

As you are becoming cognizant with clarity, the internal struggle dissipates, and is replaced with blissful serenity and joy, leading to the discovery of your true purpose and mission.

Living your true purpose is to be a bright sun, shining your light, every moment of your life. It is a state of bliss and serenity. It is forever evolving toward an ability to sustain a consciousness of the sacred and pure love for all life. From that frequency and space, your mission is unfolding and expanding. You are inviting all your gifts to be revealed in harmony to be of service to all life.

The vision of your purpose and mission is in your heart. Nurture that vision and allow it to grow in your heart. Invite a space in your heart where divine creativity expands from your purpose and mission. Your mind is naturally working with your heart. You are awakening a willingness to be of service, to uplift, and to bring increasing goodness into this world.

As a new creative path opens up, trust and know that everything unfolds always for your highest best and at the right time. Surrender to allow all flow. Find peace and appreciation in every moment.

Practice, moving effortlessly with the flow of life—free from all resistance. Trust the flow and trust the unknown. In your prayers and meditation invite God's infinite qualities of love and divine knowledge to awaken from the core of your being. Free the mind, open your heart to experience the heart of God and bask in that unconditional love. Free from all resistance, you open a space to experience boundless divine guidance and nurturing energies of love—an expanding awareness of your purpose and mission.

Move effortlessly with the flow of your life's events. Your body is relaxed, and your mind is at peace. In this new space, you experience the true reality that everything is possible and unlimited. It is a delightful, soft, loving, and nurturing flow. It is the experience of a loving, nurturing, creative power beyond all that you could even imagine. It lives within you and within all forms of life. It is a universal source of divine consciousness. It is a force expanding in infinity. You are divinely guided within that force—and you are one with it!

As you welcome within you that force of divine consciousness to guide your path, your mission is revealed and unfolds effortlessly.

Take time to contemplate the idea that you are one with all that is, sacred within the immensity of all life's sacredness, and divine within boundless cosmic divine consciousness.

When your intentions are based on goodness and love, you convey these vibrations in all your actions and thoughts, naturally projecting rays of light in all directions.

Make a list of all that gives you joy and all that you love to do. Infuse your consciousness with gratitude. Rejoice in that gratitude. Contemplate your list every day and feel the joy. Write down activities or projects you would love to welcome into your life—and describe them with joy.

Visualize creating goodness, wellness, and happiness in people's lives—and in your life.

Move your consciousness in your heart and write a list about all you would like to do to bring forth more peace, love, joy, beauty, and harmony in you, in your life, and in your environment. Make a similar list directed to the animals and Mother Nature. How can you revere, love, and nurture the animals and Mother Earth? Do something every day that brings forth more joy, wellness, harmony, hope, love, and beauty into the world. It can be an act of kindness—bringing food to a homeless, a smile, a prayer—or whatever comes to you and is of love in the moment.

As you are fulfilling your purpose, your mission is revealed.

As more ideas are birthing, complete your lists. Invite your vision to expand in the most harmonious and joyous way.

Living in true consciousness of your inner divine being is the wisdom to perceive the world without distortion. It is radiating and communicating loving goodness and kindness to all beings and life. It is a state of joy, harmony, and emotional equilibrium. It is a state of inner realization and harmonic synergy with Source, and all life, inviting your purpose and divine creative gifts to be expressed. It is your most natural state of being. You are living your gifts, guided by a higher power—the power of love.

If you still experience a void or confusion, instead of filling this void with ephemeral external illusory pleasures or addictions, find the courage to listen to that void and move into your heart. Delve into the deepest place of your being—breathe peace love light. Meditate and allow the sweet, nurturing, loving essence and presence to be revealed, dissolving all emptiness, pain, and voidness.

If you are convinced that your happiness, worthiness, and peace depend upon others, you will be endlessly disappointed. As long as you are affected by the behavior and actions of others, you are allowing ego to run your emotions and life. You are in a state of victimization, struggle, and confusion. Choose to reconnect with your true identity from within.

You will experience peace if you are free of judgment and attachment regarding anyone's actions, words, and thoughts. You cannot hold other people responsible for creating your happiness, joy, or sorrows. If you do this, you are caught in a space of illusory thoughts led by the ego. If you free everyone around you from that responsibility, you naturally free yourself too. People will feel uplifted, peaceful, and cheerful around you.

Love, serenity, and lasting happiness are within you. It is in "you" that you find this divine source and nurture it. This is who you are. Nurture that source of love in you—it is the love of God.

In the presence of God's love within you there is a sacred space of boundless divine creativity revealing your purpose and mission.

Insights about Karmic Issues

We are living the consequences of our actions and choices of consciousness at any moment. We are living the good and the bad we choose to perpetuate. This is karma.

In every moment, we project energy—and this energy comes back to us.

We have the ability to choose and practice loving-kindness. When we choose to emanate and express the highest qualities of loving-kindness and goodness in everything we do—and toward everyone—we activate a flow that holds the same vibrations. We create good karma and uplift the whole world. Everything we do and project has ripple effects.

Deep emotional wounds and traumas are usually associated with karmic issues. They are sourcing from this present life or from past lives. These wounds represent the moment when the person chose temporarily to separate from their divine Self or God consciousness within. Such wounds are usually caused by painful events. In reality, we are never separated from God. Ignoring our true spiritual nature or God-Self creates deep pain. Losing faith can create a deep gap of fear and doubt within one's being. The love life force natural flow is temporarily scattered or sporadically interrupted, creating emotional and physical pain and illness.

When are you ready to release a karmic issue?
When it is right into your face! When the pain associated with the issue is fully experienced through extreme grief, you know that you don't want to live with these painful feelings anymore—you are eager to let go of them.
When you choose to forgive and to live within the consciousness of the heart, all traumatic karmic issues are naturally released. This clear vibration invites the space for your divine presence to be experienced and lived in the moment. Our global ascension toward higher dimensions of light supports that process.

As I have explained in previous chapters, it is possible to heal these traumas by facing the pain (realizing that you are not the pain) and by transforming this pain into wisdom and compassion. The pain becomes a lesson of awareness and the lesson becomes a tool of wisdom and compassion. Moving through this shift of consciousness opens the heart—you then experience the essence of your being.

You are a ray of light in the radiance of God. You have free will to ignore that reality or to live it fully. Living in the consciousness of your divinity and light is living your purpose. Living your purpose feels good—you feel whole.

Divine Creativity

Infinite divine creativity flows from qualities of love as a natural expression of your soul. You are living your purpose and mission.

It is always through love that you empower yourself. It is always through love that you discover the infinity and multidimensionality of your creative beingness. It is always through love that you bring about peace and joy.

We are creative beings, in infinite ways. A magnetic energy naturally flows and expresses itself through us in all aspects of our lives—often without any awareness of its presence, magnificence, sacredness, and magical power.

You have the ability to invite a creative loving and divine flow in any activity, occupation, or situation. It is a consciousness of the sacred and of the heart.

As I was returning home from a three-week seminar—on energetic healing—my heart was filled with gratefulness and joy. Shortly after arriving home, I decided to take a walk in nature with my two companion dogs. I was in deep gratitude and joy—loving life! The dogs were so happy; they were

201

running and playing around me. I was in a space of the heart, embracing the sounds and energies in nature, feeling a never-ending flow of gratitude. I was embraced by waves of boundless love energy and light sourcing from everywhere. I could feel my whole beingness expanding endlessly, reaching all creation. I was experiencing pure love and blissful serenity in boundless ways. I was everywhere and everything. I was experiencing oneness. It was love consciousness—limitless and timeless!

I was experiencing a cosmic expansion of creative energies working through me. I knew this experience would stay within me forever as a blueprint—as an awakening. I also knew that these divine creative forces of love consciousness are inherently embedded within every human being and expressed consciously or unconsciously, in all space, time, and dimensions. They encompass all life and source from all life.

I was experiencing some aspects of the immeasurable vastness and multidimensionality of life.

As you awake from within, you fall in love with life. Doorways of light are activated as you align with true divine consciousness! You are allowing the highest forces of love light divine intelligence to create through you and to lead your path.

Your inner experience is born from a frequency you choose to allow, emanate, and express. It is an energy, which guides your life experience.

> *In my creativity, I experience a cosmic energetic ecstatic expansion of my whole beingness. My consciousness is expanding endlessly in joy. Divine creative visions and insights boundlessly flow with ease. They are guiding my path.*

You have the ability to experience this state of blissful creativity at any moment in your life.

When such energetic alignment occurs, all creative work carries the highest peace love light synergies and expressions. You are moving through cosmic multidimensional spectrums of colors, forms, sounds, and light. You are connecting with divine knowledge.

Divine creativity comes from the infinite qualities of the heart and the soul! In every moment you create, choose to create from love and in love! Divine creativity comes from the heart of your soul. Your soul is expressing its divine qualities.

It is therapeutic and liberating to express feelings in artistic creative ways. It liberates the soul. Artistic expression gently liberates and connects a person to the spiritual Self. The process activates a reconciliation with life and with the Self.

Artistic expression opens the soul and activates qualities of the soul. It allows a soothing, energetic divine expression of who you are. It is healing. It is liberating. It is joyful.

Artistic creative expression supports an awakening of the light bodies. Divine creativity is a natural expression and process, bridging the inner world and outer world of your beingness with harmonious nurturing sweet light and love.

Express your feelings and visions creatively, without judging. Liberate the full expression of your being through your creative expression.

Your creative freedom starts the moment you stop condemning yourself, judging yourself, or judging your work. Let go, let go, let go, and enjoy expressing your visions and emotions from your heart—without judging! Liberate the mind and create from the heart of your soul! When you express the qualities of the heart you naturally create from a higher place and with love.

Being creative is not about struggling to be perfect. Let go of the ego and liberate your creative journey! Liberate the mind and delve into the consciousness of the soul!
All feelings associated with competition, comparison, and judgments have to dissolve so that true divine creativity flows boundlessly.
In order to break down the walls of limited beliefs, we have to awaken from the heart to the sempiternal presence of the light. We have to learn

to see beyond what is. The personality is then expressing qualities from the heart. Be a conduit for love. It is divine creativity!

You have the ability to sustain divine love creative frequencies and flow, in everything you do: when you speak, think, feel, paint, write, teach, compose music, clean, cook, run, swim, conduct a business deal, interact with family and friends, or practice diverse healing modalities. All that you do can be harmonizing, blissful, and uplifting. All is of a creative frequency and process. Everything you do can be directed toward infinite goodness for yourself, all beings, and Mother Earth. Sustaining an awareness of the sacred and praise, in everything you do, activates divine creative flow and knowledge. It brings forth increasing peace on the planet.

Life is of a divine creative energy forever expanding and transcending in infinity. You have the ability to live every moment of your life in the consciousness of that divine loving creative flow.

Awakening to divine boundless creativity is experiencing a sacred union with Source—with all that is. It is inviting the soul to convey its qualities and beauty within a sacred space. It is living the sacredness of your being and the sacredness of life.

Discover Your Gifts

Allow a flow of divine creativity to be manifested through multiple expressions and unlimited facets of your being and life. Express your gifts with joy for the highest purposes of uplifting and harmonizing— and for the goodness of all life.

When the ego dominates, you are partially or completely losing the truthfulness, freedom, and clarity of your inner divine guidance. You are blocking the flow of divine creativity and the expression of your gifts. When the ego is softened, you are stepping away from feelings of insecurity and judgment. You are stepping away from illusory beliefs

204

and feelings. As a result, your divine creative abilities have space to unfold and you have the ability to express your gifts.

Your God-given gifts are revealed harmoniously from the sacred space of your heart.

Faith and complete surrendering activate the revelation of your gifts. In your faith, you have the ability to allow an endless flow of the highest creative qualities to be expressed divinely in the most surprising ways.

Faith is a state of complete surrendering, trust, devotion, and allegiance. It brings forth the divine expression of your beingness. Your whole being is moving into harmonic alignment. You are discovering your gifts.

Faith allows you be who you are. Faith is of nurturing love. It is an awareness of the soul and of the sacred.

From birth, children have free access to divine creativity, encompassing boundless gifts. They will move into adulthood sustaining that fundamental connection if the environment allows that energetic frequency and flow.
If children become indoctrinated with false, negative, and illusory beliefs while growing up, they might partially or fully lose the experience of that sacred connection until they decide to move back to true consciousness of their inner creative freedom and divinity.

As long as you are looking for answers outside of yourself—and as long as you are avoiding connecting and delving into the magnificence of your inner being—you will feel incomplete. You cannot find outside of yourself what you cannot see and live within you.

Bliss is a sacred space within you that is completely free from all attachments and earthbound thought forms. It is a place of inner freedom and pure love. In that space, divine creativity unfolds with your gifts.

As you discover and embrace the magnificence of your light being, you are inviting goodness and nurturing energies into your existence, revealing your creative gifts, purpose, and mission.

Your gifts are an expression of your divine nature. From your gifts, your purpose and mission are revealed with further clarity. Use your gifts in service to all life and create from love consciousness. You are a blessing to all life. Your gifts are unique and are sourcing from your sacred heart—the heart of creation and from oneness.

CHAPTER NINE

How to Live Your God-Given Gifts from a Place of Love, Wisdom, and Reverence

OPEN YOUR HEART AND INVITE your gifts to be revealed from the love and light of your heart—the heart of your soul. Your gifts are sourcing from God consciousness within you to serve higher purposes so that you may touch the lives of many—with blessings of love and joy—through the divine creative expressions of these gifts.

> *I honor my soul's purpose—I express truthfulness and integrity.*

Integrity is a spiritual quality that has to be consciously developed and understood. It is naturally expressed on your spiritual path. When you have integrity, you are true to yourself. You are choosing truthfulness, reverence, and honor. Integrity is of love consciousness. It is a quality of the heart and the soul.

> *I honor and value my God-given gifts from a place of integrity and divine consciousness.*

Some people fail to remember the sacredness and holiness of their

God-given gifts. When egoistic thoughts and behaviors take over, a veil of illusion is taking place, leading to a lack of awareness and a distorted view of life. People forget about the purpose and sacred aspect of their gifts. They forget to use their gifts from a place of holiness, reverence, and unconditional love. Consequently, they might use, and abuse, hurting others and themselves—without being fully aware of these patterns, in the moment.

All gifts from the Creator, reaching all aspects of life, have to be lived from the highest consciousness of love, gratitude, and reverence.

Sometimes people lose clarity and awareness about spiritual principles such as qualities of integrity and reverence in regard to their gifts. I have chosen to share the following insights since it is an issue that touches many people's lives, as well as my life. In the following insights, my intent is to bring further clarity to this subject.

For example, if you have the gift of seeing through time and space, it is important to understand that nobody is allowed in any way, to look thoroughly into anyone's life unless invited to do so by that person—or under special circumstances—it has to be authorized by Source and divine guidance—it has to serve spiritual purposes.

When you receive visions and messages, ask God with your Master guides of the light to guide you so that you may always serve the light and the highest purposes. Learn to be clear about your intentions. Give all to God and embrace God's boundless consciousness of love.

If you have healing gifts and you are helping people with diverse healing modalities, you are naturally receiving messages from Source and divine guidance. You are using these gifts to help a person who is going through painful challenges. You receive information from divine guidance in order to guide and move that person through the healing process of releasing and harmonizing energies. This process and these messages (received from divine guidance) are beautiful. They are blessings to support all healing and harmonization.

Practicing healing work using the gift to see through time and space and then invading someone's space to observe what this person is doing without being invited to do so is inappropriate, damaging, and usually causes mental and emotional distress. This behavior might engender physical health issues for both parties. To be and feel violated is always traumatic. To feel violated when you trust someone or are in pain is hurtful and distressing in any circumstance.

When we are in pain, we look for loving, healing, nurturing energies and support. For the intuitive spiritual practitioner, moving across a space that is not permitted is inappropriate and harmful. It is an invasion and a violation. Such behavior may cause negative karmic issues for the person that is doing the energetic invasion.

If you have received the gift and the ability to see and travel through time and space—with loving-kindness—contemplate thoroughly your awareness related to your sense of self-worth, integrity, and reverence. Do you violate people's space and privacy? Do you realize how hurtful it is to feel violated in this way? Have you been violated in similar ways as a child and think there is nothing wrong with it? Did you learn about integrity and respect as a child—or were they ignored in the environment you grew up? Do you know how to use your gifts with awareness, wisdom, reverence, and unconditional love? Do you know how to love yourself?

If you are violating people's space with no regard for their privacy—ignoring spiritual qualities of reverence—try to see why it is unhealthy. It is important that you stop your work to look deep within yourself for clarity, understanding, healing, and divine guidance.

Look deep within for all the repressed pain, unresolved issues, and unhealthy patterns you have been hiding from your Self.
It is possible that these unresolved issues are reflected into your life in

various ways. It is possible that you are experiencing ongoing unpleasant events and you have no idea why you are creating them. Search deep within you and look at what is really going on in your life. What are you creating and why?

Now is the time to heal and embrace nurturing love. Now is the time to move into love consciousness. Now is the time to love "you." Remember who you are!

You have the ability to let go, change, heal, and harmonize anything you wish from within your beingness. This is your gift and free will. Do not condemn yourself. Use this gift with wisdom and love. Sustain nurturing feelings. Ask God for clarity and divine guidance. Move through your realignment process with grace. In order to heal this issue, look deep within you for the place you have ignored and deprived of love. Learn to love and honor all of who you are. You will then be able to honor all beings and all of life.

If you are a spiritual practitioner and if you have received the gift and the ability to see through time and space, you can help many people who are coming to you for guidance and healing—if you have integrity, awareness, wisdom, and compassion—and if you choose to work from your heart.

Always ask for people's consent to see and hear what will guide and support the healing. This can be done through a beautiful prayer—opening a sacred space. Your prayer conveys deep respect. It serves everyone's highest purposes or aspirations and the best in all life.

Within God's love and light, ask God, your divine guidance team, and your higher Self to show you anything that is significant to supporting the healing and harmonization of the person you choose to help.

Ask God for divine guidance to lead you where you need to go, to hear what you need to hear, and to see what you need to see, in order to help this person. Always choose to express the highest qualities of compassion, reverence, love, and integrity. Through this loving process, you are learning to do God's work. You are honoring and

sustaining harmony for you, the person you intend to help, and all beings. You are then giving everything to God and you are divinely guided.

If someone comes to you for help, healing, or guidance, they will inform you about specific issues they would like to resolve and heal. Within God's light and in a sacred space, ask God and your divine guidance team to show you with clarity what you need to see and hear to support this person's harmonic realignment process—it is honoring and loving to all of life.

Choose to express reverence, respect, harmony, and boundless love so that nobody's space is violated, nobody gets hurt, and everyone is uplifted in God's love and light.

This approach teaches you about honoring who you are and all beings. It is teaching you about integrity, respect, compassion, and pure love. You are healing yourself by having this realization. You are learning to love and live in sacred ways—in every moment of your life.

When you place yourself in God's love and divine guidance, always surrender. If you are working from your heart within God's light, you will always be in harmonic alignment with goodness and the highest vibrations of love. Open your heart and allow divine guidance to show you the way. Surrender to God's loving guidance and grace.

> *I am a part of a higher force and design. It is a holy force. When I pay attention to it, accept it and embrace it, I realize that it is divine love consciousness, loving me boundlessly. I then realize that this force lives in me.*

Pay attention to the nature of your verbiage and your thoughts when you are helping and guiding someone. Stay anchored in your heart. Learn to use words with the highest vibration of love, compassion, and respect.

When people come to you for help, healing, or guidance, they are open, in pain, or vulnerable. Your feelings, your intentions, your thoughts, and your words have to express the highest energies of love—from the heart—in reverence and infinite compassion. Live the language of love and light. You are working from a consciousness of the sacred and divinely guided. You are then in alignment with your true Self.

Never violate people's trust by divulging their confidences. It is inappropriate to share people's personal stories and information—unless you have mutually agreed to do so, otherwise you may be causing harmful consequences. People will feel betrayed and violated, and rightfully so. Consequently, these people may have a difficult time to trust and seek help in the future.

Communicate with love and respect in any situation.

Throughout your life, you have the ability to make clear choices. You are in your power when you choose to emanate the highest vibrations of love, reverence, and integrity—doing God's work and living from your heart.

The moment you are clear with your choices, ascertaining your intentions and wishes in your heart and prayers, you are divinely guided. Choose to live from the highest place of integrity and pure love.

My choices and intentions are clear within my mind and heart. I live every moment in the most honoring and loving ways.

Do not try to control the healing process. Express your intentions clearly, then let go and allow divine guidance to lead the way. You are not in charge—the highest divine power, intelligence, and design of peace love light is in charge. Release your prayers in complete faith. Let them be infused and activated by the love of God. Allow and invite the healing and sacred light from an open heart. Your mind is still. You are fully present and bathing in light with the person you are helping.

You are holding a sacred space. The sacred light is working through the person you wish to help. The healing light is also emanating from your hands if you are guided to proceed with hands on healing. You are surrendering completely to invite the healing, harmonic alignment, and love light flow. You are not alone—divine beings of light are guiding you and guiding the healing. There are many hands of light proceeding with the healing and guiding you to be a clear channel.

Sustain an awareness of the sacred in all you do and toward all life. You are then projecting rays of love light around you and throughout all of creation.

If you have been betrayed or feel violated in any way, it is an opportunity to become even more conscious and loving. It is an opportunity to bring forth God's love light into your heart and life. It is an opportunity to learn to forgive, to let go, and to open your heart to feelings of mercy, compassion, and nurturing love. It is an opportunity to call upon divine assistance and to move closer to your God-Self. It is an opportunity to learn about equanimity and to become impervious to unbalanced energies.
Learn to sustain and express qualities of integrity and reverence. It is an opportunity to open your heart and embrace peace love light.
Any lesson or challenge is an opportunity to move closer to God and to be increasingly more loving and conscious.

Using your God-given gifts from a place of awareness and unconditional love opens doorways of light. You are divinely guided, uplifted, and loved by all life.

All that life is offering on all levels of our existence has to be lived with a consciousness of reverence, wisdom, and unconditional love. Love consciousness is inherently embedded as a divine design at the core essence and heart of our being. It springs from all life boundlessly.
Honor all of your God-given gifts and learn to play in the light with joy!

CHAPTER TEN

Energetic Harmonization Through Pictographic Art

A Symbolic Artistic Representation of the Tree of Life
Divine Messages Expressed and Transmitted
Creatively by Sarah Jeane

TEACHINGS AND ENERGETIC TRANSCENDENCE

A S A LIGHT WORKER, I have been divinely guided to bring forth divine creative synergies from the highest realms of light, sourcing from all dimensions and contributing to the energetic transcendence of the planet with all life—in twelve artistic representations. I have created these twelve artistic images to awaken the qualities of the heart. They are a wonderful spiritual support to this book and its messages.

This artwork is available in my book, Twelve Doorways of Light: Sacredness of Life, and on my website: artfromthelight.com.

These twelve images are doorways of light, reflecting the twelve aspects of God and divine qualities. Each of these artistic images represents one aspect of God—a powerful spiritual doorway to the light and of the light, providing energetic harmonization and light activation.

These doorways of light represent an energetic support to the written messages in this book. They sustain sacred global space in our present ascension toward higher dimensions of light.

The doorways offer a meditative support, activating the essence of the Tree of Life within, and our light body through the illuminated heart and mind. This process invites the energetic expression of the divine feminine, activating a Portal of Light to experience our God-Self.

These twelve images are leading you on a journey within all dimensions in sacredness. We are breathing and living within all twelve dimensions as well as within twenty-six dimensions—there are possibly additional dimensions. The first twelve dimensions are more consciously accessible to humankind at this time.

All dimensions are intrinsically interconnected with our beingness as well as all life. Each dimension represents specific aspects of life and purpose within the creation. They are synergistically interconnected and one with all that is, and with all twelve aspects of God.

The symbols presented in every image create a specific holy frequency related to divine qualities and correspond to every aspect of God. All symbols emanate specific spiritual resonances and esoteric significance.

These twelve images have been created within God's light, within sacred space. They mirror our divinity, our multidimensionality, and our divine oneness with all that is.

The twelve aspects of God represented in these twelve images convey a revelation of one's energetic sacred centers. They are activated by light and God's divine qualities. They bring forth the manifesting divine power of the ultimate doorway to the enchanted pathway to God:

The Tree of Life within the Flower of Life—the fundamental holy life force within all beings and within all life.

The synergy of these twelve images leads to an extraordinary portal to the most luminescent light.

How to Benefit from Twelve Doorways of Light

I am inviting you to meditate on these artistic images to support the awakening of your God-Self, the Tree of Life—the twelve Aspects of God within you. As you study this book, you may enjoy using these images as an energetic support and activation.

Since every aspect of God is represented in one image, you have the opportunity to commune on a deep level with any aspect of God and its dimension, for spiritual support and harmony, personal healing and light activation. You may meditate on any of these images to activate a specific aspect of God and divine qualities, emanating from the core essence of your being.

You may meditate on every image separately first to support the activation of every aspect of God from the heart of your being. It is awakening your body of light. As a second step, you may place them around you to invite the ultimate activation of your light body. You are inviting an experience of your God-Self. With the support of this book and its spiritual guidelines, you are stepping through a portal, leading to an experience of your God-Self.

Since all twelve aspects of God are working together in perfect harmony and oneness, I created an energetic link among all of them based on the divine science of the Tree of Life. This is why it is important to consider this creative work as a unit. Through contemplation and meditation, they naturally awaken the qualities of God within. They awaken your sacred Self.

This energetic pictorial representation of the Tree of Life epitomizes the ultimate doorway or portal to the enchanted pathway to God.

Every image represents one aspect of God illustrated with its specific color light ray, divine synergy, and dimension.

The messages within this book with the twelve artistic images provide a support to harmonize and purify all your bodies and your whole energy field. They activate your sacred energy centers and your strands of DNA/RNA with light. Your light body is awakening. You are raising your consciousness toward higher dimensions of light.

This creative work represents a divine portal in service to all humanity, in furtherance of harmony and peace on Earth—awakening peace love light in all hearts.

God's boundless love consciousness and divine knowledge are experienced by those who foster the ability to live from the heart—loving and honoring all of life.

May these messages open your heart and inspire you to believe in peace.

Prayer for Peace

I wish for all beings to believe in peace.
I wish for peace, love and harmony, ease and grace, honoring and beauty—for all beings, the world, and for me.
I wish for all beings to awaken.
I wish for harmonious abundance, prosperity and wealth, and fun—for all beings and for me.
I wish for growth and laughter—for all beings and for me.
I wish for the Earth Being and all its beauty to be held in great love and reverence, by all human beings, all beings, and consciousness.
I wish for the animals to be cherished, loved, and cared for by all human beings, all beings, and consciousness.
I wish to live in the Garden of Eden, and be lovingly nurtured by the Great Mother and the Great Father.
I wish to feel deep love and gratitude in my heart for eternity.
I wish to live in the Garden of Eden of my Heart.
I wish to be held in love, feeling so safe and nurtured, now and always.
I wish to know who I am.
I wish to live in the consciousness of who I am.
I am a ray of light of boundless love, forever held in Father Mother God's sempiternal radiance—and this is who I am!
I breathe and live in the heart of God.
I am peace love light consciousness.
I am.
And so it is.

Peace on Earth.

I am releasing into the divine light of God this sacred creative compilation in service to all humanity. This work invites and allows the space for the infinite universal paradigm of the supreme light to radiate in its full divine expression and frequency, sourcing from the Flower of Life, encompassing all elements in nature, all levels of creation and all sacred geometry.

May this creative compilation reach the most profound place of our beingness, so that in oneness, we shall open our hearts to rejoice in the Divine Living Presence!

May the highest qualities of love, reverence, compassion, joy, and gratitude be now recognized and expressed in all hearts—throughout the planet and beyond. May we live in holy consciousness, awakening infinite creative gifts and divine forces of love light sourcing from the heart—navigating within the light of the Tree of Life—to merely know oneness.

May we celebrate life in joy, everlastingly expanding in grace, forever free in the light!

About the Author

SARAH JEANE is a visionary artist and graphic artist, illustrator and art director, author, spiritual counselor practitioner, angel therapist, and spiritual teacher. She chooses to express "Light, the Sanctity of Life", in all that she creates to uplift all beings and our world.

In Europe and the U.S., after many years working in the movie industry and various companies as an art director, background artist, illustrator and graphic artist, she decided to dedicate her creative gifts to serve a higher spiritual purpose, and bring forth the light and beauty of our world.

Throughout her life, Sarah Jeane had several near death experiences. She has been embraced by the light many times and guided into higher dimensional realms of consciousness. As an empath, Sarah Jeane understands and sees people's pain and also sees and feels the joy and the light. She feels and sees energies, and communes and works with angelic beings of light. She learned to be of service by using this gift with grace and love.

Since her early twenties, she has been studying and practicing healing modalities, yoga, and meditation. This journey led her to discover her true purpose, as a clear angelic channel to serve all beings on their journey and bring forth the sacredness and beauty of our world.

Sarah Jeane created a sequel presenting pictographic art to further epitomize the essence of this compilation. This sequel book is entitled *Twelve Doorways of Light: Sacredness of Life*.

Printed in the United States
By Bookmasters